DRUM PROGRAMMING
A Complete Guide to Program and Think Like A Drummer

By Ray F. Badness
Studio Musician, B.S.E.E., M.S.E.E.
Foreword by Mark Simon

Cover
Special Thanks to:
Anita Lawhon at Radius
Michael D'Amore at Yamaha
James Catalano at Ludwig Drums

Layout and Production – Ron Middlebrook

ISBN 978-0-931759-54-3
SAN 683-8022

© Copyright 1991 by Roger W. Graham.

CENTERSTREAM Publications
P.O. Box 17878 Anaheim Hills, CA 92807
Phone/Fax (714) 779-9390 - E-Mail, Centerstrm @ AOL.com
All rights for publication and distribution are reserved. No part of this book may be reproduced in any form or by any electronic or mechanical means including information storage and retrieval systems without permission in writing from the publisher, except by reviewer who may quote brief passages in review.

This text is dedicated to the memory of my good friend Roderick Beard.

He will be deeply missed.

Contents

Foreword by Mark Simon.................... 4
Preface 6
Introduction 7

Chapter 1
The Basics

The Drum Kit................................ 8
The Drum Machine............................ 10
Song Structure.............................. 11
Real Time and Step Time Programming......... 12
Save Your Work.............................. 13
Tempo and Time Signature.................... 14
Quantization................................ 15
Drum Machine Tabulature..................... 16

Chapter 2
Kick and Snare

Kick and Snare Basics....................... 17
Programming Your First Pattern.............. 19

Chapter 3
Hi-hat and Ride Cymbals

Hi-hat Basics............................... 23
1/4, 1/8, and 1/16 Note Hi-hat Rhythms...... 24
More Hi-hat Rhythms......................... 26
Ride Cymbal Basics.......................... 31
Which Do I Choose?.......................... 32

Chapter 4
Tom-toms

Tom-tom Basics.............................. 33
What Are Fills?............................. 34
Adding a Rhythm Fill........................ 35
Adding a Tom Fill........................... 36
Playing With Quantization................... 41

Chapter 5
More Cymbals

The Crash, China, and Splash................ 44
Intro's, Bridges, and Finalés............... 45
Intro....................................... 46
Bridge...................................... 47
Finale...................................... 48
Putting It All Together..................... 49
Recapping the Process Used to Create a Drum Track... 53
Blank Drum Machine Tabulature............... 55

FOREWORD
by Mark Simon

When Ron Middlebrook of Centerstream Publishing first approached me about writing a foreword for a book on drum machine programming, I was skeptical. I thought, "who needs another book about programming drum machines, most of the tapes I hear prove that people are already quite adept at programming drum machines... *to sound like drum machines*!"

So, I read the book and was pleasantly surprised! This is not a "select pattern 22, enter edit mode B by selecting the green button labeled quantize" book. This is a book about learning to think and program like a drummer. This (in my opinion) is a very important subject.

I meet people daily who play me their tapes with incredibly simulated guitar and sax solos, great string and horn lines, but inevitably their phenomenal feats of programming are overshadowed by a a lackluster drum track, Why will many composers spend hours getting the pitch-bend on a background harmonica track just right, only to use a "preset" drum pattern? I feel the problem is simply a lack of good information to help them understand a complex instrument they do not play. That's where this book comes in. Ray has taken a direct and mathematical approach to teaching you drumming. I like that he gives you solid guidelines in which to work, not "rules set in stone".

When I was a working session drummer, and I would get a call from a producer I had never worked with before, I would try to find other albums and projects he had done to become familiar with what he looked for in a drummer. I would then go to the session ready to simulate what I *thought* he wanted in a drummer. However, in many instances after the first pass he would tell me that I played *too* simple or there were *too* many fills, or what ever the style was I had heard in his previous work. He would then explain that he "had hired me for *my skill and reputation as a creative drummer*, not as a drum machine", and that "if he had wanted the same stuff again, he would have hired the same drummer". The point to this story is not to say, "don't bother doing your homework, because doing *my homework* kept me working as a *session drummer* for many years. The point to this story is to "use your creativity".

As Ray points out, go by what your ears tell you. If it sounds good, DO IT! If it doesn't, go back and try again. By following this book you can get an understanding of the drum kit that takes many drummers years to learn. In this age of technology, with sampling and computer assisted performance, it's easy to think our drum programming and sequencing sound "real" when compared to *other programming*. But remember a drum machine is an "emulation" of a drum kit, so strive to be as creative as a "human drummer" not a "preprogrammed drummer".

Have fun with this book and may you hear many times upon its completion my favorite question about my drum machine tracks, "Who played the drums?, you used a drum machine?!"

BIO

Mark Simon was a "session drummer" for many years playing on countless record, T.V., and demo projects before becoming a full-time composer. Although he currently doesn't earn his living as a drummer, Mark continues to play "real drums" for enjoyment and composing new rhythmic ideas. Because after all, drum machines cannot be creative, (yet) they can only play what you give them. Garbage in = Garbage out, Cool ideas in = Cool ideas out.

I would like to express a special thank you to the following persons for their unfailing support during this long and cumbersome project:

Rick Bilheimer
Scott Lewis
Steve McEntee
Dan Bertolucci
Rich Adams
Chris Dunker
Marq Ligman
Dan Polidi
John Riley
John Hanlon
Steve Wilson
Peter Doctors
and
Tom Graham

Thank you gentlemen.

Preface

Learning to program a drum machine can be both confusing and frustrating. My first experience was no exception. No matter how hard I tried, I could not manage to get the machine to play the rhythms I heard in my head. This was partly because I couldn't play a real drum kit, and partly because I didn't have the six years of college needed to program the model I had. Thoroughly confused and broke from my so called "investment", I set out for college to solve all my problems......or so I thought.

During my years at college, I searched high and low for a book such as this one. One that was geared toward the novice user and could explain both the basics of drumming and drum programming in 100 pages or less. I'm still looking for that book. Luckily, you've just found it.

Ray F. Badness

Introduction

The complexity of most drum machines makes them difficult, if not downright confusing to operate. To make matters worse, the owner's manuals have a tendency to assume that the reader is familiar with sheet music, song structuring techniques, and the rudiments of drumming. This couldn't be a worse assumption since many people who own drum machines are self taught musicians who cannot read sheet music or play a real drum kit. This text will therefore present material in such a manner that no music theory or drumming background is required.

Each chapter of this text will explore a different piece of drum hardware, including how it is played, and how it is programmed. In addition, short exercises throughout the book will further exemplify the concepts presented and produce a sample song when completed. Probably the most important aspect of this text is that you need not be able to play a drum rhythm with your hands in order to program. Programming will be taught using a play by number system that is so simple, anyone can learn. In a nutshell, all of the basic instruction you will need to master the art of drum programming lies in the following pages.

Realistic drumming techniques will be the focus of this text for two reasons. First, they will save you money. How? Drummers with ten arms aren't very easy to come by. Consequently, your first world tour will be quite expensive when you have to hire five drummers to play what you've haphazardly programmed. Second, lawsuits over sampling are common. You cannot possibly get yourself into trouble if you do your own drumming. Besides, anyone can digitally sample a drum riff from an old James Brown or Van Halen record. Be both original and cost effective at the same time; do your own drumming.

If you haven't done so already, read or skim through your owner's manual to get a basic understanding of how your machine operates. It is not necessary that you master all of its operations, just take a few moments to recognize the many functions that it can perform and note some of the most common keystrokes used such as pattern creation, pattern clearing, tempo adjustment, time signature specification, and quantization change. There is no question that you will not understand everything the first time around. That is hopefully where this text will fill in the gaps. In just a few hours you will be well on your way to making great music and having great fun.

As a precautionary note, you will need 42 empty patterns in your drum machine to complete this text. Check your machine and verify that patterns 01 through 42 are indeed empty. If they are not, consult your owner's manual for the specific keystrokes required to clear them. Good luck!

-Chapter 1-

The Basics

The Drum Kit

Drums, cymbals, sticks......now what? Confusion! Drummers make it look so easy. Their seemingly effortless motions impose an aura of magic over a drum kit. Similarly, a *"good"* martini also seems magical, but in actuality, the methods used to master both are really quite simple (only simple in thought however). The critical and most difficult part is the physical motion. This is the part that takes years to master and consequently, is the magic.

Upon first glance, drumming may seem to be complex because of the number of different motions and amount of gear involved. But upon closer inspection, you will notice that certain rituals are repeated over and over for generic outcomes. Let me try and put it in perspective for you. When you get up in the morning, why do you go to work? Because you need to catch up on your sleep? Well, some do, but most people go to work because they need money. The ritual here is work, and the outcome is money. Drumming is much the same. When you want a bare bones basic drum beat, play the Kick Bass, Snare, and Hi-hat. When you want to accent a note or chord in your music, strike the Kick and a Cymbal at the same time. When you want to speed up your music, play faster. I think you get the picture. Honestly, the only complex part of drumming is disciplining your hands and feet to play different rhythms at the same time.

The modern day musician has therefore been confronted with a modern day dilemma; to be or not to be a real drummer. A real kit takes years to master. To gracefully pound it with all four limbs and look smooth at the same time is a real challenge. Not only this, but finding a place to practice can also be a time consuming venture. On the other hand, all of this pain and suffering can be bypassed for a few hundred bucks, this text, and a pair of headphones. Yes, once again modern electronic technology has prevailed. For a fraction of the cost of a real kit, a drum machine will allow you to own a digital sample of most every piece of drum hardware in existence. But, although the price of a drum machine is right, none of the current models can *"identically"* mimic a real drummer, yet! Nevertheless, it's an alternative that must be considered given the fact that drum machines have been steadily improving.

Most modern day drumming uses patterns borrowed from the past. In this sense, half of your work has already been done for you. All you have to do is repeat history. For this reason, as we make our way through this text, you are sure to recognize many of the patterns. This is yet one more example that drumming is not that difficult.

Figure 1 shows a typical drum kit. Let's take a look at its composition. Notice that every kit will contain at least one Kick, a Snare, Cymbals, and Tom-toms. Generally, the **Kick** and **Snare** are used to set the basic beat of the pattern. The **Hi-hat** cymbals, although omitted by some programmers, are crucial to include because they add a realistic feel and rhythm to the overall sound. The remaining **Cymbals** (Crash, China, Splash, etc...) are often used to accentuate climactic peaks and valleys in the music. And lastly, the **Tom-toms,** or Toms, are most commonly used for fills which will be discussed in great detail in Chapter 4. Keep in mind that these are only rough guidelines and should be taken accordingly.

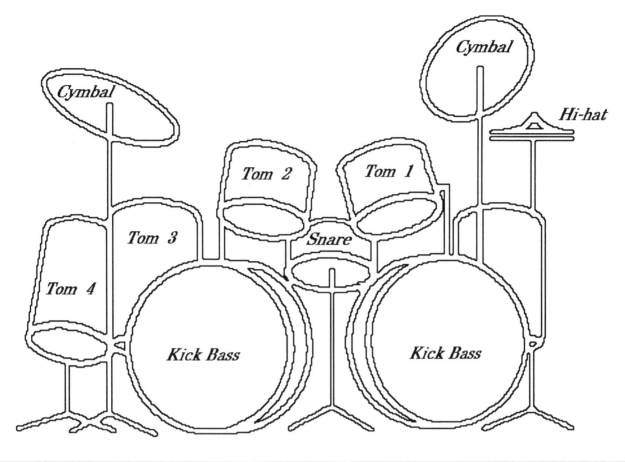

Figure 1 : The Drum Kit

As we've just discussed, each piece of drum hardware has a musical purpose. You will generally find that each is struck with a repeating pattern and force. Probably the most important thing to remember is that a drummer has only two hands and two feet. Since you too have only four limbs, obviously there is a limit as to how many pieces you can strike at one time.

In general, a basic drum rhythm will entail controlling the amount of Hi-hat separation with your left foot, and producing the Kick Bass rhythm with your right. Your left hand strikes the Snare drum, and the right strikes the Hi-hat. It is important to note that the Snare will be on your right and the Hi-hat on your left (your right arm crosses over the left to strike the Hi-hat). Notice that only three pieces of drum hardware are used. The Kick Bass, Snare, and the Hi-hat. Also notice that it takes all four limbs to control them. However, your arms and legs are not confined to this configuration. Just about anything is possible. As you will see in Chapter 3, the right hand can also be used to strike the Ride Cymbal instead of the Hi-hat. I encourage you to be creative when programming and experiment with the hardware at your disposal. Figure 1 will help you picture realistic arm motions.

Keep in mind that your drum rhythms should theoretically match your music. If this statement confuses you, take a closer listen to your favorite records. Listen to the way the Kick and Snare rhythm compliments the music. You will find that there is a definite correlation between the strum of the guitar and the rhythm that the Kick and Snare produce. If there is no guitar in your music, you will find that this correlation occurs with another instrument. In Rap music for example, the syllables in the lyrics follow the Kick and Snare rhythm. For now, just keep this in mind. We'll talk more about how to do this in Chapter 2.

The Drum Machine

Today's drum machines are of superb 16 bit audio quality and contain standard features that could only be dreamt of ten years ago (human feel, automatic drum fills, MIDI, etc...). Whereas it was excusable to sound awful with the first generation of drum machines, today there is no excuse for bad drum programming.

Over the last decade, drum programming has found its way into almost every genre of music. From the music we hear on our radios and televisions, to the P.A.'s at our local night clubs, it's everywhere. For those of us who know how to program, it's music to our ears, but to the live drummer it must surely seem to be a forecast for extinction.

Fortunately, no one is becoming extinct, including the live drummer. Not only are his techniques and methods in great demand by us, the programmers, but he also has something that our modern electronics will never replace...his human essence. Would you pay to see a band with no human members? I rest my case. It's terribly more exciting to watch humans perform than to listen to a box full of electronics spit out pre-programmed data. On the other hand, if you were a record producer interested in keeping recording costs to a minimum, you would surely opt for the box full of electronics. What's my point? There is plenty of room in the world of music for drummers and drum machines. In fact, they are both necessities!

What is a drum machine? A drum machine is a computer whose sole purpose is to facilitate the recording and playback of drum rhythms. It is different from a personal computer (PC) in two regards; one, it has drum sounds stored inside of it, and two, it has a built in sequencer. That is not to say that a personal computer cannot be configured to play drum rhythms. Quite to the contrary, it is entirely possible. However, it costs a significant amount of money to buy the sequencing software, MIDI interface, and sound source. If you are short on cash, a drum machine will get you the most bang for your buck.

What does a sequencer do and where do the drum sounds come from? A sequencer does just what you might guess. It allows the composer to arrange sounds and patterns in any sequence, then play them back as arranged. As for the drum sounds, they are merely digital samples stored on memory chips inside the machine.

What is a digital sample? A digital sample is a non-continuous approximation of an analog sound. In plain English, an analog sound is the real thing, or in our case, the one that emanates from a drum when hit. As for a digital sample, think of a *"connect the dots"* puzzle in a child's game book. By drawing a line through the dots placed on a page, you can create a picture. This picture is not the real thing, but it's so close that anyone can tell what it is. Digital sampling is a similar process of storing audio dot locations in memory. When played back, they sound very close to the original, so close in fact that it's hard, if not impossible, to tell the difference.

As you might imagine, if there were more dots on your page, your picture would look much better. Theoretically, with a very large number of dots placed very close together, the dots would appear to form the picture without having to connect them. So how do you electronically put more dots on a page? Take a higher bit sample. I'm sure you have heard of 12 bit or 16 bit samples? Higher bit samples have improved audio quality, just as more dots on a page make a better picture. For this reason, 16 bit samples sound better than 12 bit. It is interesting to note that the current electronic technology will allow sampling in excess of 16 bits. Unfortunately, your ear probably wouldn't be able to hear the difference and most musicians wouldn't be able to afford it.

As you can imagine, the first commercially available drum machines were dramatically different than those available today. They drew heckling and disgust from live drummers, and for good reason. To say that they sounded phony is putting it mildly. Not only this, but most contained barely enough memory to program a few elaborate, non-repetetive songs. This meant that if the user were to perform for any extended period of time, he would either have to repeat patterns often, or take frequent breaks to reload the memory of the machine. This was all compounded by the fact that memory cartridges were expensive and only available for some machines. These early drum machines also had reputations for being very unreliable. System crashes, or failures, were common. As with any budding technology, time was needed for perfection.

Today, perfection is near. Not only do the most recent machines sound more realistic than ever before, but they all support a standardized set of MIDI (Musical Instrument Digital Interface) features. These standardized MIDI features enable them to talk to one another and to other MIDI equipped devices. This ability has many applications including but not limited to, syncing your drum patterns to taped music, triggering samples existing in other machines, transferring and storing your machine's memory onto floppy or fixed disk, and remote starting and stopping of other machines. Please refer to your local library or book store if you wish to find out more about the applications and protocol of MIDI. There have been many excellent books written on the subject, and you will surely wish to explore them after mastering the art of drum programming. Keep in mind that knowledge of MIDI is not required in order to program your drum machine.

Song Structure

Your song structure will make or break your song. However, if you wish to forge into the nineties by breaking traditional song structures, skipping this section will be your destiny.

If it is pop stardom you desire, your songs should generally last between 3 and 4 minutes. Longer compositions will tend to do one of two things; bore the listener, or overexpose your catchiest passages. As they say, too much of a good thing can be detrimental. When in doubt, leave the listener wanting more. Along the same line, instrumental sections are fine, but 12 minute solos may also bore the listener.

As for the title of your song, something so simple could never be more important. If you've ever gone into a music store in search of a recording but been unable to find it because the lyric line stuck in your mind had absolutely nothing to do with the song title, you know what I mean. Theoretically, by taking your song title from the catchiest passage of your tune, you will allow the listener to immediately locate it when in doubt. Let me show you what I mean. I'll give you a few song titles and you see if you can remember the melody. "**Sweet Home Alabama**" - *Lynyrd Skynyrd*, "**Lucille**" - *Kenny Rogers*, "**Rhinestone Cowboy**" - *Glenn Campbell*. These are all songs that we love to hate but the song title immediately brings to mind the catchiest passage. This of course translates into additional record sales, which of course means more money for the writer (i.e. you).

All songs are comprised of blocks that fit together in many ways. These blocks are known as the *Verse*, *Chorus*, *Bridge*, *Intro*, and *Finalé*. The Intro is used to begin the song, and the Finalé is used to end it. The portion of your song that repeats over and over is called the Chorus. Likewise, the part that does not repeat, or vocal story telling portion, is done in the Verse. A Bridge is used to smooth the transition between Chorus and Verse and vice versa. Your song may or may not need one. However, if a transition doesn't sound pleasing, that is probably a good indication that you do.

A musical unit known as a *Measure*, or *Bar*, is used to define the length of a music block. A measure will vary in time duration depending on the time signature and tempo of the music. In 4/4 time, which we will discuss later, one measure consists of 4 beats, each one quarter note in length. Don't worry if you don't understand the music theory, drum machines and sequencers know how long a measure lasts. They automatically determine its length when you specify the tempo and time signature to them. Since most all music is written in 4/4 time, this leaves only one thing for you to specify which is the tempo. The upcoming section entitled *Tempo and Time Signature* lists approximate tempos for a few styles of music. You may wish to increase or decrease these to suit your needs.

In most well structured songs, you will generally find that the length of a Chorus or Verse will be a multiple of 8 bars. For example, a 16 bar Verse and 8 bar Chorus are quite common. Why multiples of 8 bars? It just seems to sound best when done in this fashion. To say that you cannot do otherwise is quite to the contrary. I encourage creativity and new thinking. Intro's and Finalés can be short (1 or 2 bars) or long (8 or 16 bars), just remember not to bore the listener and to keep the overall song time around 4 minutes. Likewise, the length of a Bridge is completely arbitrary, but generally one or two bars are used.

The solo is generally played over the music of a Verse. Note that it can also be played over a Chorus or any bit of music you desire, but the standard lengths are 8, 16, or 32 bars depending on skill and the situation. A good rule of thumb is to limit your solo to the length of a Verse.

Keep in mind that composing a song is not an instantaneous process. It will take time to explore different ideas and song structures. Experiment with the guidelines that have been presented and don't give up until it sounds the way you want. Your persistence will pay off.

There have been many successful song structures over the years. Here are a few of them listed in Table 1.

Table 1 : Song Structures

SONG STRUCTURES

Structure A	Structure B	Structure C	Structure D
Intro	Intro	Intro	Intro
Verse #1	Verse #1	Chorus	Chorus
Chorus	Bridge	Verse #1	Verse #1
Verse #2	Verse #2	Chorus	Bridge
Chorus	Chorus	Verse #2	Chorus
Intro	Verse #3	Chorus	Verse #2
Solo	Chorus	Bridge	Bridge
Chorus	Solo	Solo	Chorus
Chorus	Chorus	Chorus	Solo
Finalé	Chorus	Chorus	Bridge
	Finalé	Chorus	Chorus
		Fade	Chorus
			Finalé

Note that there are many possible variations and combinations of these structures. Mix and match! Also, you are not restricted to end your song with two or more Choruses.

Real Time and Step Time Programming

There are two ways to program a drum machine: *Real Time* and *Step Time*. Real Time programming is more complex than Step Time and requires playing the drum pattern you desire while the machine records your motions. This method can be frustrating for a non-drummer who doesn't know what he wants to hear, let alone how to play it. As a matter of fact, this method is so difficult for beginners that I recommend using Step Time Mode exclusively until you get a good feel for the machine. Step Time programming, which I like to call *"play by number"*, involves dividing a measure into an equal number of pieces of time, then placing sounds on numbers. It is very simple and will allow composition without actually playing, programming of faster fills, and easy deletion of closely spaced sounds. In the end, I think you will find that the most efficient method of programming will be a mixture of both.

Note : These two modes may have slightly different names depending upon the manufacturer of your machine. See your Owner's Manual for specifics.

Save Your Work

I can't stress this enough. Save your work frequently! As with all micro-computers, there is a tendency to crash just when you've finished your best work (Murphy's Law). You will find that some drum machines operate very erratically when 95% or more of the memory is used. If you must operate in this area, save frequently and be prepared for the worst.

Most drum machines will allow memory storage to an expensive external memory cartridge, or to a cassette. It takes a lot longer to save to cassette, but for the price you can't beat it. If you are programming a drum machine and have a personal computer (PC) available, check your music software manuals because some sequencing software will allow you to do a bulk memory dump and store data on your hard drive. This is much faster than saving to cassette, and much cheaper than a memory cartridge. If you do not own a personal computer there is another way to save your data quickly. For a few hundred bucks you can purchase a portable floppy drive. This unit represents a somewhat large initial investment, but keep in mind that floppy disks can be purchased inexpensively and can hold quite a large amount of data. As a side note, if you are using a personal computer to sequence your drum programming, make a backup copy of your sequencing files. Believe me, you'll be happy you did when your hard drive fails.

I can't help but remember my first drum machine crash. I had been blindly punching buttons for three months and had somewhat perfected 10 songs. I was just making some final changes to the drum patterns for a gig the following week when "all of the sudden", the machine started going through its start-up routine. After it finished, to my extreme disappointment, I discovered everything was gone. Everything! Three months of work vanished into thin air in only a few seconds. Maybe you can relate or have experienced this kind of extreme disappointment. While I was hyperventilating, my concerned roommate called the paramedics because he "thought" I was going into shock.

When the fire truck arrived, the paramedics asked me, "What happened?" I felt so stupid saying my drum machine crashed. Here were six paramedics expecting a heart attack victim. Finally, with great reluctance I said, "My drum machine crashed", trying to retain what little bit of self esteem I had. As you can imagine, the laughter that ensued was the best these men had had all week.

Let this be a lesson to you. My machine completely cleared itself to the factory showroom state in seconds, through no fault of my own! As a result, we didn't play the gig the following week, or the week after. I thought things would be different if I bought a new drum machine. Yah, you guessed it. That one crashed too, but this time I was ready for it.

Save your work!

Tempo and Time Signature

Drum machines have limitations as to how fast or slow they will play your music. On the low end, it's generally around 50 beats per minute and on the high end, around 250. As you might guess, the tempo of a style of music will vary greatly depending on the artist. I have listed the approximate tempos for various styles of music in Table 2. You may wish to increase or decrease these tempos to suit your needs. In any case, they will give you a place to start.

Table 2 : Suggested tempos for various styles of music.

Style of Music	Tempo (beats / minute)
Slow Rock and Country	*50 - 100*
Rock, Metal, Pop, Country, Hip-Hop, House, Funk, and Industrial	*100 - 150*
Fast Rock and Country	*150 - 200*
Slow Punk Rock	*250*

The time signature of your music is also very important. Most music on the radio and television is 4/4 time. It is the single most popular time signature used today. Even though most drum machines will allow you to play in a variety of time signatures, I think you will find 4/4 the easiest. For this reason, all patterns in this book are written for the 4/4 time signature.

What does 4/4 stand for? The numerator represents the number of beats per measure and the denominator represents the note given a value of one beat. In this signature there are 4 beats per measure with a quarter note carrying the value of one beat. Simply put, 1 measure = 4 beats = 4 quarter notes or *4 x 1/4 = 4/4 = 1*. Complete understanding of this concept is not crucial. What is important is that the time signature of your drum machine is set to 4/4 when programming any patterns in this text.

Quantization

I know you've heard this word before and wondered what it meant. Quantization is a fancy word for dividing a measure into an equal number of pieces of time. For 8 pieces you will need 1/8 quantization. For 16 pieces you will need 1/16 quantization. I think you get the picture.

One sixteenth quantization will be used as the standard in this text because it lends itself nicely to programming todays popular drumming techniques including, double kick bass and 1/16 note hi-hat rhythms.

Table 3 contains a listing of some standard quantizations for most drum machines. It is there to illustrate an important concept. Notice that if you are programming in 1/8 quantization and change to 1/16 quantization, the numbers on which notes appear, will change respectively. For example, if you have a Snare on numbers 3 and 7 in 1/8 quantization, they will move to 5 and 13 in 1/16 quantization. Don't worry, the pattern will sound exactly the same. The only change will be the number of pieces that the measure is divided into. In this case, we are doubling the number of pieces so the note locations must move to accommodate this change. This is mentioned here for an important reason. If you ever change quantization while programming, you may be confused when your notes move to different numbers. Now you won't, but just in case we'll do an example in Chapter 4.

Table 3 : Quantization Table

Quantization	One Measure
1/4	1 2 3 4
1/8	1 2 **3** 4 5 6 **7** 8
1/16	1 2 3 4 **5** 6 7 8 9 10 11 12 **13** 14 15 16
1/32	1 2 3 4 5 6 7 8 9 10 11 12 13 14 15 16 17 18 19 20 21 22 23 24 25 26 27 28 29 30 31 32
1/96	

Why would you ever want to change quantization? Well, imagine you are about to fight the Heavyweight Champion of the World. First, let me say I hope you have a nice funeral. Second, if you had your choice of throwing 8 punches every second or 16, which would you choose? Stupid question right? Well obviously, when fighting The Champ, you would like to get in many punches as quick as possible because you may not be standing for very long. On the other hand, let's say you're fighting some Hollywood movie chump like *Rocky*. You'll probably only need 8 punches per second to take him down. Drumming is very similar. Sometimes you may want the sticking (arm motion) in your fills to happen faster, just like punches. 1/8 Quantization may be fine for slow fills, but for those faster fills you may want to go to 1/16, or 1/32 quantization. The only drawback with going to a smaller quantization is that it takes more time to step your way through all the numbers in Step Mode. 1/16 quantization will minimize your stepping time and at the same time allow programming of fast or slow fills when you need them. You will see this later in Chapter 4 when we discuss fills.

Drum Machine Tabulature

The drum machine *tabulature* used in this book may seem confusing at first glance, but don't worry. It is quite simple to understand because it is presented in a format *anyone* can read. Here's how it works.

Table 4 contains two measures of drum programming. The drum kit hardware to be used is listed down the far left column. The drum machine pattern number in which to place your drumming is listed at the top of the hardware column. Depending upon the quantization, you will see a different number of columns per measure. For example, in 1/8 quantization, you will see 8. In 1/16 quantization, you will see 16. Table 4 contains 16 columns, thus we have 1/16 quantization. Column number 1 represents the beginning of the measure and 16 the end. Three different letters will be placed under the column numbers to designate when and how a piece of hardware is to be played. They are, **A - accent**, **F - flam**, and **X - marks the spot**. Placement of an unaltered drum sound is denoted by an X (thus marking the spot). In other words, wherever you see an X, place one note of that drum sound on the designated number. The **A** in the following tabulature represents an accented note. In this case, not only would you place a note on the designated number, but also slightly increase its volume (typically +6 on a scale of 1 to 100). Some machines are equipped with an ACCENT button for exactly this purpose. Simply hold it down while entering the note you wish to accent. Since many machines do not have an ACCENT button, consult your Owner's Manual if you are unsure. If yours doesn't, note that the volume of an individual note may also be altered by editing its level parameter while in the *edit pattern mode*. (This mode is used to edit the parameters of any sound after it has been placed in a pattern. Again note that not all manufacturers will call this function by this exact name, so consult your Owner's Manual.) If you cannot accent individual notes, replace the A with an X and move on. An **F** in the following tabulature represents a flam. A flam occurs when a drum head is struck with both sticks a split second apart. This is a very common and important technique used in most all drumming styles, yet some drum machines do not have this feature. If your machine does not, there is a way to do it without one. We'll discuss this technique later in Chapter 4 since it involves changing quantization and may be a little overwhelming at this point. For now, consult your Owner's Manual and replace the F with an X if you are unable to flam.

> *The following pattern is intended only as an example of the tabulature used in this text. It is not expected that you enter it into your drum machine.*

Table 4: Drum Machine Tabulature

00	1st Measure																2nd Measure															
	1	2	3	4	5	6	7	8	9	10	11	12	13	14	15	16	1	2	3	4	5	6	7	8	9	10	11	12	13	14	15	16
Kick Bass	A						X			X			X				X		X	X			X	X								X
Snare					X							X									X				F		F			X	X	X

-Chapter 2-

Kick and Snare

Kick and Snare Basics

Let's discuss some very fundamental concepts regarding the Kick and Snare drums. If you are already familiar with what they are and how they are played, you may wish to skip ahead two paragraphs.

Kick drums come in various sizes and are generally located on the floor facing toward the drummer. As the name implies, foot and leg motion are used to depress a mallet clad pedal which strikes the face of the drum. Although tonality is a function of size, tuning, electronic signal processing, and what is stuffed inside of them, generally, larger diameter drums have a lower pitch than smaller.

The Snare drum on the other hand, is usually hit with a stick or brush. Although one could use just about anything including his/her hands, head, or feet, most drum machine samples were produced using a stick. The Snare also varies in tonality depending on the location of the stick impact, tuning, and electronic signal processing.

Because the Kick and Snare are the backbone of every drum rhythm, you should lay them down first when composing your patterns. How do you do this? As we will discuss later, the Snare is placed on the same numbers of every measure (5 and 13 in 1/16 quantization). The Kick however, takes a little more thought. Ideally, you would like to come up with a rough idea for your song first (i.e. rhythm guitar lick). Then, taking note of the rhythm of your strum, correlate the Kick rhythm with it. When composing your pattern, your goal should be to make most every strum fall on either a Kick or a Snare. Trial and error is the key here since you may find that some on and some off add a nice touch. The primary concern is to merely find a rhythm that compliments your music. Similarly, if you are programming Rap music, you would like to correlate the Kick and Snare rhythm with the syllables of the lyrics. As always, these generalizations merely represent a good starting point for your drumming creativity. If confusion is still abound, listen closely to the drumming in your favorite songs. Analyze and take note of the way the Kick and Snare rhythm matches the music. This will surely answer many of your questions.

Before composing a Kick and Snare rhythm, it is necessary to decide which of the many samples inside of your drum machine that you will use. This process is similar to color coordinating your clothing in the morning. While a turtle neck sweater may look absolutely phenomenal with a pair of polyester pants, combining it with a pair of paisley Bermuda shorts results in a fashion atrocity. Remember, beauty is in the eye of the beholder so choose a Kick and Snare that *you* feel not only sound good together, but also fit your music.

Matching a drum rhythm with your music will most likely be a trial and error process in the beginning. In fact, it will probably be easier to come up with a drum rhythm first, then put music to it.

This is not a very efficient way to go about writing a song though. This is because you will most likely produce bits and pieces of music that may or may not sound good when fit together. The solution lays in the programming methods of this text and practice.

On that note, let's discuss a couple of rules of thumb to keep in mind when composing patterns. First, *do not make your patterns any longer than two Bars.* *(Note: Some drum machines will ask you to specify your pattern length in beats as opposed to Bars. This is not a problem since 4 beats = 1 Bar in 4/4 time. For 2 Bars, specify 8 beats.)* The problem here is that your drum machine does not contain an infinite amount of memory and you will use it up very quickly. Manufacturers do this because, one, memory is expensive, and two, they would like you to by their expensive memory cartridge. For these reasons, optimize your memory use. Two Bar patterns will do a very good job of this. Consequently they will be used exclusively throughout this text. Also keep in mind that most all song parts are generally a multiple of two Bars. For this and countless other reasons, you cannot go wrong using this rule of thumb. Second, *the Snare is always placed on numbers 5 and 13 of each measure when using 1/16 quantization.* *(Note: Some drum machines utilize different numbering schemes when in Step Mode. The numbers are not 1 through 16, but instead based on the beat number of the measure. Don't let this throw you. If you have a machine that uses this convention, keep in mind that there are 4 beats per measure in 4/4 time. For this reason, the numbers may start with either a 1, 2, 3, or 4 and be followed by a slash and another number. Each of the 4 beats per measure will be divided and numbered in accordance with the quantization selected. For example, if you select 1/16 quantization you will get 16 numbers per measure each representing a discrete space on which to place a sound.)* Once again, sixteenth quantization means that each measure is divided into sixteen equal pieces of time. Notice that no matter how you slice it, the numbers 5 and 13 are eight numbers apart. This translates into a regular and repeating snare beat.

Changing quantization can be a frustrating experience if you do not have a complete understanding of the concept. The Snare, and all other sounds for that matter, will change numbers respectively as you change quantization. Each pattern will sound the same, however the respective number on which each note appears will change. For example, if the Snare appears on 3 and 7 in 1/8 quantization, it will move to 5 and 13 in 1/16 quantization. Likewise, it will move to 9 and 25 in 1/32 quantization. Refer to Table 5 and note that these pairs of numbers all represent the same moments in time.

How did I determine where the Snare would appear? It's simple. Let's take 1/16 quantization for example. To get the first number, multiply the denominator of the quantization by 1/4 and add 1 ((16 x 1/4) + 1 = 5). The second number is attained in a similar fashion. Multiply the denominator of the quantization by 3/4 and add 1 ((16 x 3/4) + 1 = 13). I told you it was easy. Using this mathematical algorithm you will always know where the Snare will be for the quantization you are in. For simplicity sake, Table 3 has been reprinted as Table 5 to remove the need for the mathematical calculation as shown.

Table 5 : Quantization Table

Quantization	One Measure																															
1/4	1							2								3								4								
1/8	1				2				3				4				5				6				7				8				
1/16	1		2		3		4		5		6		7		8		9		10		11		12		13		14		15		16	
1/32	1	2	3	4	5	6	7	8	9	10	11	12	13	14	15	16	17	18	19	20	21	22	23	24	25	26	27	28	29	30	31	32
1/96																																

Since the Snare repeats over and over at equal intervals, it is therefore up to the Kick to produce the different sounding rhythms. This is how the drums are matched to your music. In Step Mode, all it takes is a little trial and error to find the numbers that translate into the rhythm you hear in your mind. With a little practice, you will soon be able to make an educated guess where to place the Kicks for the rhythm you want.

Placing a Snare on numbers 5 and 13 is a good starting point for most drum rhythms. However, you may wish to add more Snares, especially if you are programming Rap rhythms. In a case such as this, try 8 and/or 10 in addition to 5 and 13 for a more funky feel.

It is very common today to find two Kick drums in a drum kit. Most drum kits of yesteryear had only one. As you can imagine, with only a single Kick, drummers were limited in both speed and rhythms. Double Kick, or two Kick drums, allow the drummer to produce faster, more diverse Kick rhythms because there are two bass drums, one for each foot. Unfortunately, this also creates a dilemma. Namely, it requires removing the left foot from the Hi-hat pedal in order to play the second Kick. Because of this, you will find that some drummers have 2 Hi-hats, one locked in the closed position, and one unaltered as before. This in turn allows the drummer to play the Hi-hat in the closed position without having to remove his left foot from the second Kick to depress the pedal. Of course, this whole process adds to the complexity and cost of drumming, but the sound makes the sacrifice worthwhile.

Double Kick is not hard to master with a drum machine. In fact, you probably would have discovered it on your own if I didn't tell you. In 1/16 quantization, all you have to do is place the Kicks on adjacent numbers and increase the tempo. For ear pleasing reasons, it is not advisable to place sixteen Kicks in a row. Place them next to each other, here and there, or wherever you find produces a rhythm to your liking. Experimentation is the key. For example, placing Kicks on numbers 7, 9, 10, and 11 and increasing the tempo to around 150 will do the trick. You will see how simple it is in the next section when we key in our first patterns.

Note that a real drummer will vary the amount of force applied on each Kick. This is easily remedied in our case by increasing the volume of some of the Kicks slightly. Consult your Owner's Manual for specific instruction on editing single note parameters. Typically, increasing the volume level by +6 on a scale of 1 to 100 will improve realism greatly. Experimentation is the key here.

You may also wish to vary the pitch of your Kicks. As you can imagine, a real drummer cannot perfectly tune both of his Kicks to exactly the same pitch as you can with your drum machine. For this reason, if you vary the pitch of your Kicks slightly, you may notice an even greater increase in realistic sound.

Programming Your First Pattern

Consult your Owner's Manual for instruction on pattern creation if you are not already familiar with your machine. Most drum machines will ask you to specify the length of your pattern before you start. ***Two Bars*** will be the standard length for all patterns in this book, so if you must, specify 2. Again note that some drum machines will ask you to specify your pattern length in beats. If this is the case, use *8 beats* since 4 beats = 1 Bar in 4/4 time. You will also wish designate the time signature at which you will be working. Again, all patterns in this book are written for ***4/4 time*** (Note that this is the default time signature for most drum machines so you can probably skip this step). As for tempo, designate ***115 beats per minute***. Don't forget, some drum machines utilize different numbering schemes when in Step Mode. The numbers are not 1 through 16, but instead based on the beat number of the measure. Don't let this throw you. If you have a machine that uses this convention, keep in mind that there are 4 beats per measure in 4/4 time. For this reason, the numbers may start with either a 1, 2, 3, or 4 and be followed by a slash and another number. Each of the 4 beats per measure will be divided and numbered in accordance with the quantization selected. For example, if you select 1/16 quantization you will get 16 numbers per measure each representing a discrete space on which to place a sound.

Exercise 1: Our first pattern will be very basic. This brings to mind an important point. Songs do not have to be complex to be good. On the other hand, simplistic drum programming can lead to monotony so use your ears as the final judge.

Pattern 01 is just about as simple as you can get. In each measure it has a Kick on 1 and 9, and a Snare on 5 and 13. Before entering it into your drum machine, make sure the quantization is set to 1/16. After you have entered Step Mode and verified that there are 16 spaces, place Kicks on 1 and 9, and Snares on 5 and 13 of each measure. If you make a mistake, consult your Owner's Manual for note clearing instructions and try again.

01	1st Measure																2nd Measure															
	1	2	3	4	5	6	7	8	9	10	11	12	13	14	15	16	1	2	3	4	5	6	7	8	9	10	11	12	13	14	15	16
Kick Bass	X								X								X								X							
Snare					X								X								X								X			

Note: This may seem so intuitive that it need not be said, but this pattern (or any pattern for that matter) will not sound right if the sounds are not placed on the correct numbers. If the Step Mode numbers do not go up to 16, or if you do not have 16 discrete spaces on which to place your sounds, something is wrong. Consult your Owner's Manual if this is the case. Correct quantization and number placement are imperative.

After entering Pattern 01 into your drum machine, exit Step Mode and listen to your creation. Notice that the pattern is quite simple and will go with just about anything, all you have to do is adjust the tempo. If you are like me though, it's just not complex enough. For this reason, you will find 12 more patterns on the following pages that are of varying complexities and among my favorites.

Exercise 2: Enter each of the following patterns into your drum machine. In doing so, you will begin to get a feel for placing Kicks to produce the rhythm you are searching for. Patterns 4, 6, 7, and 11 will resemble double Kick if the tempo is increased to approximately 150. Your efforts will not be wasted here because all of these patterns will be used in the Hi-hat exercises of Chapter 3.

02	1st Measure																2nd Measure															
	1	2	3	4	5	6	7	8	9	10	11	12	13	14	15	16	1	2	3	4	5	6	7	8	9	10	11	12	13	14	15	16
Kick Bass	X								X								X								X	X		X				
Snare					X								X								X								X			

03	1st Measure																2nd Measure															
	1	2	3	4	5	6	7	8	9	10	11	12	13	14	15	16	1	2	3	4	5	6	7	8	9	10	11	12	13	14	15	16
Kick Bass	X								X		X						X								X			X				
Snare					X								X								X								X			

04

	1st Measure																2nd Measure															
	1	2	3	4	5	6	7	8	9	10	11	12	13	14	15	16	1	2	3	4	5	6	7	8	9	10	11	12	13	14	15	16
Kick Bass	X		X			X				X				X							X					X		X	X			
Snare					X								X								X								X			

05

	1st Measure																2nd Measure															
	1	2	3	4	5	6	7	8	9	10	11	12	13	14	15	16	1	2	3	4	5	6	7	8	9	10	11	12	13	14	15	16
Kick Bass	X		X			X	X			X			X				X		X			X		X		X					X	
Snare					X								X								X								X			

06

	1st Measure																2nd Measure															
	1	2	3	4	5	6	7	8	9	10	11	12	13	14	15	16	1	2	3	4	5	6	7	8	9	10	11	12	13	14	15	16
Kick Bass	X								X					X			X		X	X			X			X		X			X	
Snare					X								X								X								X			

07

	1st Measure																2nd Measure															
	1	2	3	4	5	6	7	8	9	10	11	12	13	14	15	16	1	2	3	4	5	6	7	8	9	10	11	12	13	14	15	16
Kick Bass	X		X	X			X		X			X			X				X	X			X	X		X		X			X	
Snare					X								X								X								X			

08

	1st Measure																2nd Measure															
	1	2	3	4	5	6	7	8	9	10	11	12	13	14	15	16	1	2	3	4	5	6	7	8	9	10	11	12	13	14	15	16
Kick Bass	X		X					X	X								X		X						X				X			
Snare					X								X								X								X			

09

	1st Measure																2nd Measure															
	1	2	3	4	5	6	7	8	9	10	11	12	13	14	15	16	1	2	3	4	5	6	7	8	9	10	11	12	13	14	15	16
Kick Bass	X								X				X						X				X	X							
Snare					X								X								X								X			

10

	1st Measure																2nd Measure															
	1	2	3	4	5	6	7	8	9	10	11	12	13	14	15	16	1	2	3	4	5	6	7	8	9	10	11	12	13	14	15	16
Kick Bass	X								X								X		X				X				X					
Snare					X								X								X								X			

11

	1st Measure																2nd Measure															
	1	2	3	4	5	6	7	8	9	10	11	12	13	14	15	16	1	2	3	4	5	6	7	8	9	10	11	12	13	14	15	16
Kick Bass	X						X	X	X		X				X				X	X			X		X		X				X	
Snare					X								X								X								X			

12

	1st Measure																2nd Measure															
	1	2	3	4	5	6	7	8	9	10	11	12	13	14	15	16	1	2	3	4	5	6	7	8	9	10	11	12	13	14	15	16
Kick Bass	X		X				X				X				X		X		X				X				X					X
Snare					X								X								X								X			

13

	1st Measure																2nd Measure															
	1	2	3	4	5	6	7	8	9	10	11	12	13	14	15	16	1	2	3	4	5	6	7	8	9	10	11	12	13	14	15	16
Kick Bass	X						X				X								X								X	X				
Snare					X								X								X								X			

-Chapter 3-

The Hi-Hat and Ride Cymbals

Hi-hat Basics

Importance of the Hi-hat to realistic programming cannot be overemphasized. Not only does it influence the tempo of your song, but it also adds realistic feel and rhythm. Depending on how you play it, you can attain a wide variety of effects, some of which you will see as we make our way through this chapter. Now granted, your Hi-hat patterns may sound a little hokey at first, but by playing around with the attack, decay, and level of each individual note you will be able to make a large difference in the overall sound. Depending on your machine you may or may not be limited in this area so consult your Owner's Manual for specifics.

To a non-drummer, use of the Hi-hat is confusing and cumbersome. Elaborate compositions are difficult and not very intuitive. To make matters worse, most drum machines have terribly unrealistic samples. This is why you will find that many programmers refuse to use it. In most cases, you will find that owning a newer model drum machine will help, but in all cases you will have to work extra hard to obtain a realistic sounding Hi-hat.

For a non-drummer to understand how the Hi-hat is played, a firm grasp of how each sound is made is vital. Once the operation is understood, all it takes is a few hours of MTV and a little imagination to program the popular Hi-hat rhythms heard on radio and television today.

Ideally, you would like to have at least four Hi-hat samples in your drum machine. However, in some cases you will be forced to settle for fewer. The desirable four are the *Hi-hat Pedal*, *Closed Hi-hat*, *1/4 Open Hi-hat*, and *Open Hi-hat*. Let's examine them one at a time.

> The ***Hi-hat Pedal*** sound is simply the result of slamming the two Hi-hat cymbals into one another. The top cymbal will come down and eventually meet the bottom one if the foot pedal is depressed far enough. There is no sticking involved in this operation.
>
> The ***Closed Hi-hat*** is similar. This sound is achieved by striking the outer edges of the Hi-hat cymbals while they are sandwiched together (closed). Your foot is required to hold the pedal down during this operation.
>
> Striking the outer edges of the two Hi-hat cymbals while they are in their normal resting position (wide open) will produce the ***Open Hi-hat*** sound. There is no foot motion involved here.
>
> And lastly, the ***1/4 Open Hi-hat*** sound is made by depressing the Hi-hat pedal until the two cymbals are, you guessed it, 1/4 open. At this point, the outer edges are hit with a stick.

Remember that it is going to take practice to know which one of these to use and when. Don't get discouraged though, if you put in the time, the sound of your music will reflect it.

1/4, 1/8, and 1/16 Note Hi-hat Rhythms

The Hi-hat can be played at many different tempos. Interestingly, the speed you play it influences whether the pattern sounds fast or slow. A drummer will most commonly use three speeds. They are quarter, eighth, and sixteenth note rhythms. Music theory isn't important here. What is important is that when we're done, you understand how to enter each of these 3 different rhythms into your drum machine. Let's do an example.

First, we must select a Hi-hat sample for use in our patterns. Our choices include the Hi-hat Pedal, Closed Hi-hat, 1/4 Open Hi-hat, and Open Hi-hat. Choose the 1/4 Open Hi-hat if you have it. If not, do the following exercises with the Closed Hi-hat. As for a Kick and Snare rhythm, we have 13 excellent choices from Chapter 2 (Patterns 01 - 13). Choose Pattern 02. In the following three exercises we will add the aforementioned Hi-hat rhythms to Pattern 02 then compare the results.

Exercise 3: Let's start with a quarter note rhythm. Copy Pattern 02 to Pattern 14 in your drum machine. This is done so that if by some remote chance Pattern 14 gets screwed up, Pattern 02 can be recopied. Now enter Step Mode and place a *1/4 Open Hi-hat* (or Closed Hi-hat if you do not have it) everywhere shown to make your Pattern 14 appear as follows.

Pattern 14   **Quarter Note Hi-hat Rhythm**

14	1st Measure																2nd Measure															
	1	2	3	4	5	6	7	8	9	10	11	12	13	14	15	16	1	2	3	4	5	6	7	8	9	10	11	12	13	14	15	16
KickBass	X								X								X									X		X		X			
Snare					X								X									X								X			
Hi-hat Pedal																																	
Closed Hi-hat																																	
1/4 Open Hi-hat	X				X				X				X				X				X					X				X			
Open Hi-hat																																	

Notice that the Hi-hat appeared on numbers 1, 5, 9, and 13. These are all 4 apart. Why? This is because 1/4 (1/4 note rhythm) = 4/16. Hence, a quarter note equates to 4 apart in 1/16 quantization.

24

Exercise 4: Now let's create an eighth note rhythm. Copy Pattern 02 to Pattern 15 and modify it to appear as follows.

Pattern 15 — Eighth Note Hi-hat Rhythm

15	1st Measure																2nd Measure															
	1	2	3	4	5	6	7	8	9	10	11	12	13	14	15	16	1	2	3	4	5	6	7	8	9	10	11	12	13	14	15	16
Kick Bass	X								X								X									X		X			X		
Snare					X								X									X								X			
Hi-hat Pedal																																	
Closed Hi-hat																																	
1/4 Open Hi-hat	X		X		X		X		X		X		X		X		X		X		X		X		X		X		X		X	
Open Hi-hat																																	

Notice that the Hi-hat appeared on numbers 1, 3, 5, 7, 9, 11, 13, and 15 this time. These are all 2 apart. Why? This is because $1/8$ (1/8 note rhythm) = $2/16$. Hence an eighth note equates to 2 apart in 1/16 quantization. I think you get the picture.

Exercise 5: Let's finish the lesson by creating a sixteenth note Hi-hat rhythm. Once again copy Pattern 02, this time to Pattern 16. If you wish, you may copy Pattern 15 to Pattern 16 instead. This will reduce the number of Hi-hats you will have to enter when editing Pattern 16. Reconfigure Pattern 16 to appear as follows using whatever method you wish.

Pattern 16 — Sixteenth Note Hi-hat Rhythm

16	1st Measure																2nd Measure															
	1	2	3	4	5	6	7	8	9	10	11	12	13	14	15	16	1	2	3	4	5	6	7	8	9	10	11	12	13	14	15	16
Kick Bass	X								X								X									X		X			X		
Snare					X								X									X								X			
Hi-hat Pedal																																	
Closed Hi-hat																																	
1/4 Open Hi-hat	X	X	X	X	X	X	X	X	X	X	X	X	X	X	X	X	X	X	X	X	X	X	X	X	X	X	X	X	X	X	X	X
Open Hi-hat																																	

At this point, I think you know why there are Hi-hats on every number between 1 and 16. I also think you have heard the difference between the three patterns. Notice that even though the Kick and Snare rhythm did not change, the change in Hi-hat tempo made Pattern 16 sound faster than Pattern 14.

In actuality, a real drummer will utilize many different Hi-hat sounds when playing a rhythm. In the next section we will bring in the three other Hi-hat samples and examine their use.

In 1/16 quantization, a 1/16 note Hi-hat rhythm will have a Hi-hat on every number between 1 and 16, a 1/8 note rhythm will have one every 2, and a 1/4 note rhythm will have one every 4.

More Hi-hat Rhythms

Now that we've got 1/4, 1/8, and 1/16 note rhythms under our belt, let's create some new rhythms by combining all of the Hi-hat samples inside of your drum machine. Keep in mind that your Hi-hat patterns will most likely sound a little hokey when compared with the real thing, but if you play around with the attack, decay, and level of each individual note in your pattern, you'll be surprised at the difference you can make. Limitations in this area may become apparent with older drum machines.

There are no rules in songwriting, only patterns that sound good when played. Do not let the patterns I am about to present confine your creativity. They are only a basis from which to build your drumming technique. Analyze them, experiment, and challenge yourself, because after all, that is what will set you apart from everyone else.

Exercise 6: You will notice a trend in the following patterns; ***The Open Hi-hat is almost always accompanied by a kick of the bass drum.*** That is not to say that on every Kick, an Open Hi-hat should be placed. More clearly, if you use the Open Hi-hat sample, you *may* wish to place a Kick on the same number. Experiment.

Twelve more Hi-hat rhythms appear on the following pages. Enter Patterns 17 through 29 into your drum machine by copying the respective Kick and Snare patterns from Chapter 2, then adding the Hi-hats.

Copy Pattern 02 to Pattern 17, then add Hi-hat to Pattern 17.

Pattern 17   1/4 Open and Open Hi-hat

17	1st Measure																2nd Measure															
	1	2	3	4	5	6	7	8	9	10	11	12	13	14	15	16	1	2	3	4	5	6	7	8	9	10	11	12	13	14	15	16
KickBass	X								X								X									X		X		X			
Snare					X								X								X									X			
Hi-hat Pedal																																	
Closed Hi-hat																																	
1/4 Open Hi-hat		X	X	X	X	X	X	X		X	X	X	X	X	X	X		X	X	X	X	X	X	X		X		X	X			X	X
Open Hi-hat	X								X								X									X		X		X			

Copy Pattern 03 to Pattern 18, then add Hi-hat to Pattern 18.

Pattern 18   1/4 Open and Open Hi-hat

18	1st Measure																2nd Measure															
	1	2	3	4	5	6	7	8	9	10	11	12	13	14	15	16	1	2	3	4	5	6	7	8	9	10	11	12	13	14	15	16
KickBass	X								X	X							X					X				X							
Snare					X								X								X									X			
Hi-hat Pedal																																	
Closed Hi-hat																																	
1/4 Open Hi-hat			X		X		X		X					X		X			X		X			X		X			X			X	X
Open Hi-hat	X												X				X					X				X							

26

Copy Pattern 04 to Pattern 19, then add Hi-hat to Pattern 19.

Pattern 19 — **Closed and Open Hi-hat**

19	1st Measure																2nd Measure															
	1	2	3	4	5	6	7	8	9	10	11	12	13	14	15	16	1	2	3	4	5	6	7	8	9	10	11	12	13	14	15	16
Kick Bass	X	X			X			X			X								X			X	X		X	X					
Snare					X								X								X								X			
Hi-hat Pedal																																
Closed Hi-hat	X			X			X				X						X			X					X	X					X	
1/4 Open Hi-hat																																
Open Hi-hat			X			X			X				X						X			X							X			

Copy Pattern 05 to Pattern 20, then add Hi-hat to Pattern 20.

Pattern 20 — **1/4 Open and Open Hi-hat**

20	1st Measure																2nd Measure															
	1	2	3	4	5	6	7	8	9	10	11	12	13	14	15	16	1	2	3	4	5	6	7	8	9	10	11	12	13	14	15	16
Kick Bass	X	X			X	X			X			X					X	X			X	X	X								X	
Snare					X								X								X								X			
Hi-hat Pedal																																
Closed Hi-hat																																
1/4 Open Hi-hat		X	X	X		X	X	X		X	X	X	X	X			X	X	X		X	X	X		X		X	X	X			X
Open Hi-hat	X				X				X				X								X				X	X				X		

Copy Pattern 06 to Pattern 21, then add Hi-hat to Pattern 21.

Pattern 21 — **Closed and Open Hi-hat**

21	1st Measure																2nd Measure															
	1	2	3	4	5	6	7	8	9	10	11	12	13	14	15	16	1	2	3	4	5	6	7	8	9	10	11	12	13	14	15	16
Kick Bass	X								X							X	X		X	X			X		X		X				X	
Snare					X								X								X								X			
Hi-hat Pedal																																
Closed Hi-hat	X		X		X		X		X		X		X									X		X			X		X		X	
1/4 Open Hi-hat																																
Open Hi-hat															X		X					X										X

Copy Pattern 07 to Pattern 22, then add Hi-hat to Pattern 22.

Pattern 22 — 1/4 Open and Open Hi-hat

22	1st Measure																2nd Measure															
	1	2	3	4	5	6	7	8	9	10	11	12	13	14	15	16	1	2	3	4	5	6	7	8	9	10	11	12	13	14	15	16
KickBass	X		X	X			X		X			X			X				X	X			X	X		X		X			X	
Snare					X								X								X								X			
Hi-hat Pedal																																
Closed Hi-hat																																
1/4 Open Hi-hat		X	X	X		X	X	X		X	X	X	X	X			X	X	X	X		X	X							X	X	X
Open Hi-hat	X				X				X						X						X		X		X		X					

Copy Pattern 08 to Pattern 23, then add Hi-hat to Pattern 23.

Pattern 23 — 1/4 Open and Open Hi-hat

23	1st Measure																2nd Measure															
	1	2	3	4	5	6	7	8	9	10	11	12	13	14	15	16	1	2	3	4	5	6	7	8	9	10	11	12	13	14	15	16
KickBass	X		X						X		X						X		X			X			X							
Snare					X								X								X								X			
Hi-hat Pedal																																
Closed Hi-hat																																
1/4 Open Hi-hat	X				X				X				X				X				X				X				X			
Open Hi-hat																																X

Copy Pattern 09 to Pattern 24, then add Hi-hat to Pattern 24.

Pattern 24 — 1/4 Open and Open Hi-hat

24	1st Measure																2nd Measure															
	1	2	3	4	5	6	7	8	9	10	11	12	13	14	15	16	1	2	3	4	5	6	7	8	9	10	11	12	13	14	15	16
KickBass	X								X				X				X				X		X									
Snare					X								X								X								X			
Hi-hat Pedal																																
Closed Hi-hat																																
1/4 Open Hi-hat		X	X	X	X	X	X	X		X	X	X	X		X	X	X	X		X	X	X		X	X	X	X	X	X		X	X
Open Hi-hat	X								X				X								X				X					X		

Copy Pattern 10 to Pattern 25, then add Hi-hat to Pattern 25.

Pattern 25 — **Closed and Open Hi-hat**

25	1st Measure																2nd Measure															
	1	2	3	4	5	6	7	8	9	10	11	12	13	14	15	16	1	2	3	4	5	6	7	8	9	10	11	12	13	14	15	16
Kick Bass	X								X								X	X				X				X						
Snare					X								X								X								X			
Hi-hat Pedal																																
Closed Hi-hat			X		X		X			X		X		X	X	X			X		X				X			X			X	X
1/4 Open Hi-hat																																
Open Hi-hat	X								X								X				X				X							

Copy Pattern 11 to Pattern 26, then add Hi-hat to Pattern 26.

Pattern 26 — **1/4 Open and Open Hi-hat**

26	1st Measure																2nd Measure															
	1	2	3	4	5	6	7	8	9	10	11	12	13	14	15	16	1	2	3	4	5	6	7	8	9	10	11	12	13	14	15	16
Kick Bass	X						X	X	X			X			X			X	X			X		X		X					X	
Snare					X								X								X								X			
Hi-hat Pedal																																
Closed Hi-hat																																
1/4 Open Hi-hat			X	X			X	X	X			X			X			X	X			X		X		X					X	
Open Hi-hat	X				X								X				X				X								X			

Copy Pattern 12 to Pattern 27, then add Hi-hat to Pattern 27.

Pattern 27 — **Closed, 1/4, and Open Hi-hat**

27	1st Measure																2nd Measure															
	1	2	3	4	5	6	7	8	9	10	11	12	13	14	15	16	1	2	3	4	5	6	7	8	9	10	11	12	13	14	15	16
Kick Bass	X	X			X				X			X				X	X	X			X				X							X
Snare					X								X								X								X			
Hi-hat Pedal																																
Closed Hi-hat	X				X				X			X					X				X				X			X				
1/4 Open Hi-hat																														X	X	X
Open Hi-hat			X				X			X					X	X							X			X					X	X

Copy Pattern 13 to Pattern 28, then add Hi-hat to Pattern 28.

Pattern 28 — Open Hi-hat

28	1st Measure																2nd Measure															
	1	2	3	4	5	6	7	8	9	10	11	12	13	14	15	16	1	2	3	4	5	6	7	8	9	10	11	12	13	14	15	16
Kick Bass	X						X				X								X							X		X				
Snare					X								X								X									X		
Hi-hat Pedal																																
Closed Hi-hat																																
1/4 Open Hi-hat																																
Open Hi-hat	X				X				X				X				X				X				X				X			

Copy Pattern 05 to Pattern 29, then add Hi-hat to Pattern 29.

Pattern 29 — 1/4 Open and Open Hi-hat

29	1st Measure																2nd Measure															
	1	2	3	4	5	6	7	8	9	10	11	12	13	14	15	16	1	2	3	4	5	6	7	8	9	10	11	12	13	14	15	16
Kick Bass	X	X				X	X			X			X				X	X				X	X			X			X			
Snare					X								X								X								X			
Hi-hat Pedal																																
Closed Hi-hat																																
1/4 Open Hi-hat		X	X	X		X	X	X		X	X	X	X				X				X				X				X			
Open Hi-hat	X				X				X				X																			

If you find it hard to program the Hi-hat rhythm you hear in your mind, try imagining that you are watching a real drummer play it. In your mind, picture the Hi-hat separation. This will clue you in on which sample to use. Picture the time at which he/she hits it (quarter, eighth, or sixteenth notes) and with what force. This will tell you on which numbers to place the Hi-hat as we discovered earlier in the chapter.

Ride Cymbal Basics

The Ride is a cymbal as are the Hi-hats, Crash, and China. It has a different shape and sound though. Although it can be hit anywhere, there are basically two regions that are most often played; the *center* and the *edge*. The *center* is cup shaped and when hit, sounds much like a bell. For this reason you will find it listed as either **Bell** or **Cup** in most drum machines. The other region, or the outer *edge* of the Ride cymbal, vaguely resembles the sound of tapping your car hood with the radio antenna. (I do not recommend trying this at home. Only insured professionals should attempt this risky maneuver.) This unique tone will generally be listed as **Edge** or **Ride**.

Both regions of the Ride cymbal are played with much the same hand rhythms as the Hi-hat, but usually only with one hand. Both the Hi-hat and Ride are not usually played at the same time, but they can be. Here again, physical limitations should constrain your programming. If it sounds like it takes three arms to play, it probably will.

In the next exercise, we will punch in a Kick and Snare rhythm that has not yet been entered into your drum machine. Then, just as with the Hi-hat, we will compare quarter, eighth, and sixteenth note Ride cymbal rhythms with it.

Exercise 7: Enter the following three patterns into your drum machine, and as with the Hi-hat, listen to the difference.

30	1st Measure																2nd Measure															
	1	2	3	4	5	6	7	8	9	10	11	12	13	14	15	16	1	2	3	4	5	6	7	8	9	10	11	12	13	14	15	16
Kick Bass	X		X	X			X				X								X						X		X	X				X
Snare					X								X								X								X			
Hi-hat Pedal																																
Closed Hi-hat																																
1/4 Open Hi-hat																																
Open Hi-hat																																
Ride (cup)	X				X				X				X				X				X				X				X			
Ride (edge)																																

Copy Pattern 30 to 31 and make the following changes.

Pattern 31   Eighth Note Ride (cup)

31	1st Measure																2nd Measure															
	1	2	3	4	5	6	7	8	9	10	11	12	13	14	15	16	1	2	3	4	5	6	7	8	9	10	11	12	13	14	15	16
Kick Bass	X		X	X			X				X								X						X		X	X				X
Snare					X								X								X								X			
Hi-hat Pedal																																
Closed Hi-hat																																
1/4 Open Hi-hat																																
Open Hi-hat																																
Ride (cup)	X		X		X		X		X		X		X		X		X		X		X		X		X		X		X		X	
Ride (edge)																																

Copy Pattern 31 to 32 and make the following changes.

Pattern 32   **Sixteenth Note Ride (cup)**

32	1st Measure																2nd Measure															
	1	2	3	4	5	6	7	8	9	10	11	12	13	14	15	16	1	2	3	4	5	6	7	8	9	10	11	12	13	14	15	16
Kick Bass	X		X	X			X			X									X						X		X	X			X	
Snare					X								X								X								X			
Hi-hat Pedal																																
Closed Hi-hat																																
1/4 Open Hi-hat																																
Open Hi-hat																																
Ride (cup)	X	X	X	X	X	X	X	X	X	X	X	X	X	X	X	X	X	X	X	X	X	X	X	X	X	X	X	X	X	X	X	X
Ride (edge)																																

Again notice that the 1/16 note rhythm makes the overall pattern sound faster.

Which Do I Choose?

With all of these choices (1/4 Open Hi-hat, Open Hi-hat, Closed Hi-hat, Hi-hat Pedal, Ride cup, and Ride edge), how do you decide what to use and when? Well, besides what sounds best to your ear, there is a simple rule of thumb. ***Use either the Open Hi-hat, Ride cup, or Ride edge in your Chorus. And for the Verse, use any of the Hi-hats, but not the Ride cup or Ride edge.*** This rule is not etched in stone, but is followed quite often in many songs. Use it where it sounds best. Elsewhere, I encourage you to be creative.

There is one more special tip I would like to pass on. ***Many times you will come up with a section of music and put drums to it, but not know whether to use it as a Chorus or Verse. In times such as these, I let the drum machine decide. If the music sounds best with the Ride cup, I use it as a Chorus. Likewise, if the Hi-hat compliments the music best, I use it as a Verse.***

-Chapter 4-

Tom-toms

Tom-tom Basics

Tom-toms, or Toms for short, resemble a Snare drum in basic shape. This shape resemblance does not equate to tonal equivalence however. Indeed the two sound very dissimilar. Physical differences in shell thickness and construction give the Tom-tom a hollower, rounder tone. Not only are the Tom-toms constructed differently, but they are also available in a wider variety of sizes. Diameters can range from the size of your fist, to the size of a car tire. As you might expect, a larger diameter will bring a lower pitch. The remainder of a Tom-tom's audio qualities are a function of its length, tuning, and electronic signal processing. For these reasons, you will find a large array of Tom-tom samples in your drum machine. Some resemble the real thing, while others fall nothing short of synthetic.

Any number of Toms can be found in any given kit, however the total number is generally a function of the drummer's wallet size, show, and skill. Most drum machines on the other hand, have only about four Tom samples. Each sample gets its name from its location in a left to right series. An example of what you might find is: Tom 1, Tom 2, Tom 3, and Tom 4, where Tom 1 is the highest pitched and farthest left of the series. Likewise, Tom 4 is the lowest, and farthest right. Some drum machines will follow an opposite convention where Tom 1 is the lowest pitched, so check the samples inside of your drum machine to determine which convention is used. *This text will assume Tom 1 to be the highest and consequently farthest left. If your machine does not follow this convention (i.e. Tom 1 is the lowest pitched), simply reverse the Tom numbers when completing the following exercises.*

Most real drummers would gasp at the thought of never using the Tom-toms. Yet, many drum programmers do this very thing. This can be attributed to a wide variety of reasons, some of which include:

1) **Producing a good sounding Tom-tom fill is difficult when you have no idea how to create one.**

2) **Some Tom-tom samples leave much to be desired in the way of tonal appeal.**

3) **Some styles of music simply do not utilize much Tom drumming, such as Rap, House, Hip-Hop, or Industrial. Noncoincidentally, all of these styles are dominated by drum programming.**

All of the above are valid justifications, but they are also reasons to learn. This chapter will therefore be devoted to the use of Tom-toms in their main application, a fill.

What are Fills?

Fills are short sections of drumming that differ from the basic drum pattern. What does that mean? Well, rather than boring the listener by repeating a 2 bar pattern for 4 minutes, short sections of different drum rhythms are inserted (hence the name "fill") to break up repetition and form semi-climactic peaks and valleys. They can be as simple as changing the Kick and/or Hi-hat rhythm at or near the end of a measure (a Rhythm Fill), or as complex as pounding every piece of hardware at your fingertips for a minute and a half (a Solo). The complexity is up to you, however, I think you will find that simplicity and complexity both have their moments. As a general rule, the sound of your music should take priority over the skill rating. On the other hand, the more complex your drumming is, the less it will sound programmed.

How long does a fill last? Well, that is completely up to you and basically depends on what sounds best in your song. *Most commonly, a fill will last 1/8, 1/4, 1/2, or 1 measure.* At any rate, *one is always placed during the last measure of the Verse and Chorus.* (When in 1/16 quantization, an 1/8 measure fill starts on the number 15 and ends on 16. A 1/4 measure fill starts on 13 and ends on 16. A 1/2 measure fill starts on the number 9 and ends on 16, and a 1 measure fill starts on the number 1 and ends on 16. Again, the size of your fill doesn't matter much. What matters is what sounds best in your song.)

Have you ever heard someone speak in monotone? This is how your drumming sounds if you do not use fills. In order to speak with expression you've got to vary your tone and accent the important phrases. Accent and differentiate the various blocks of your song by varying the drumming. For example, *when transitioning between Verse and Chorus, and vice-versa, place a fill during the end of the last measure.* To explain further, if your Verse is 16 measures long, place some sort of fill during the end of the 16th measure. It could involve the Snare, Kick, Toms, Hi-hat, Cymbals, all of the above, or anything you desire. Even silence can add a nice twist, but by placing some sort of fill at the end of the last measure, you will vary the tone and help lead into the next section of music.

The end of the last measure is not the only place you should use fills. As a general rule of thumb, place them at the end of every fourth bar. Now obviously, you do not want your song to sound like one big drum solo, so be selective about the size and tone of your fills. *Place large fills at the junctions of major song blocks such as the Verse and Chorus, and save the small fills for mid-Verse, mid-Chorus, etc...*

A "Small" fill implies 1/4 or 1/8 measure long. It could amount to an extra sticking of the Snare at the end of a measure. It could also translate into a change in the Kick rhythm (Rhythm Fill), or a change in the Hi-hat rhythm. It could involve combining a Kick and a Cymbal crash (we'll discuss the methods of Cymbal placement in Chapter 5). A fill can be anything you desire, or nothing at all (silence). Use your imagination, but keep your fills fairly simple when programming smaller ones.

If you repeat the fill used at the end of Verse #1, at the end of Verse #2, that's perfectly fine, but keep in mind that a real drummer will tend to vary his fills throughout a song. Although this isn't an absolute requirement, if you can do this, you are approaching mastery of the art of drumming and drum programming.

As a general rule of thumb, Rhythm fills are placed at the end of the 4th and 12th bars in a 16 bar Verse. Snare and/or Tom fills (fills composed mainly of Snare and/or Tom notes) are placed at the end of the 8th and 16th. Note that this equates to some sort of fill, no matter how small, being placed at the end of every 4th bar. For this reason, when all else fails, place a rhythm fill at the end of every 4th bar. Keep in mind that although the aforementioned do not have to be that long or that way, they are a good place to start.

Adding a Rhythm Fill

Once again, a Rhythm Fill is a change in the Kick and/or Hi-hat rhythm at or near the end of a measure. As mentioned before, you can never go wrong by placing them at the end of every 4th measure since they will serve to break up the repetition of your programming and give it more of a realistic feel. I'll show you what I mean.

Exercise 8: Let's create a Rhythm Fill for use with Pattern 29 of Chapter 3. Copy Pattern 29 to Pattern 33. Note that Pattern 33 will contain the Rhythm Fill (after you have edited it of course). Enter Step Mode and change the second measure of your Pattern 33 to appear as follows. If you wish, punch the whole pattern in from scratch if you find it easier.

Pattern 33 — Rhythm Fill

33

	1st Measure																2nd Measure															
	1	2	3	4	5	6	7	8	9	10	11	12	13	14	15	16	1	2	3	4	5	6	7	8	9	10	11	12	13	14	15	16
Kick Bass	X		X			X	X			X			X			X	X		X		X		X			X	X	X		X		
Snare					X								X								X								X			
Hi-hat Pedal																																
Closed Hi-hat																																
1/4 Open Hi-hat		X	X	X		X	X	X		X	X	X	X	X			X				X				X				X			
Open Hi-hat	X				X				X				X																			
Ride (cup)																																
Ride (edge)																																
Tom 1																																
Tom 2																																
Tom 3																																
Tom 4																																

After you have successfully entered Pattern 33 into your drum machine, play Patterns 29 and 33 in succession. Hear the difference? Notice that by following one with the other, a non-monotonic 4 bar rhythm is produced. Even though the Rhythm Fill is subtle, it adds realism and expression. Keep this in mind when your patterns sound dead or monotonous.

Patterns 29 and 33 will be used as the basis for the Verse of our song in this text. Why a Verse? As discussed in Chapter 3, since the 1/4 Open Hi-hat is used, they would probably sound best in a Verse environment. Again, you do not have to follow this rule of thumb in your songs. It is only a guideline to fall back on in times of indecision.

Adding a Tom Fill

Rhythm Fills are nice for subtle variations in your drum rhythms, but if you would like something with a little more punch, complexity, and expression, consider a Tom Fill. In the next exercise, we will compose a fill comprised of Snare and Tom notes that encompass 1/2 of a measure. As mentioned earlier, a fill can last as long as you wish. However, in a Verse or Chorus environment, it should generally include or occupy the end of the last measure.

Exercise 9: Once again, let's use Pattern 29 to precede a two bar pattern containing a fill. This time, the Pattern containing the fill will be number 34. To create it, copy Pattern 29 to 34 and modify 34 to appear as follows. Again, deletion of differing notes may be more trouble than it is worth, so if you wish, enter the following pattern from scratch.

Pattern 34 — Tom Fill

34	1st Measure																2nd Measure															
	1	2	3	4	5	6	7	8	9	10	11	12	13	14	15	16	1	2	3	4	5	6	7	8	9	10	11	12	13	14	15	16
KickBass	X	X			X	X		X		X			X		X		X	X		X		X		X		X	X	X			X	
Snare					X								X									X				X	X			X		X	X
Hi-hat Pedal																																
Closed Hi-hat																																
1/4 Open Hi-hat		X	X	X		X	X	X		X	X	X	X	X			X			X												
Open Hi-hat	X				X				X						X																	
Ride (cup)																																
Ride (edge)																																
Tom 1																																
Tom 2																																
Tom 3																													X	X		
Tom 4																															X	X

As mentioned earlier, a 1/2 bar fill begins on the number 9 and goes through the end of the measure (16). *(Note, 9 through 16 encompass 8 pieces, or 1/2 of the measure.)* Theoretically, a fill could involve placing notes on any or all of the numbers between 9 and 16. This is where your personal creativity comes in.

Although you may not realize it, we have now completed one half of a 16 bar Verse. Play the following patterns in succession and listen to what you've done so far.

Pattern 29
Pattern 33
Pattern 29
Pattern 34

Keep in mind that when composing a Verse or Chorus for your own song, the approach should be the same; *Compose a two bar pattern first, then copy it to different numbers and add fills.*

In a very short time, many patterns will be chained together. It may be awkward to play all of them in succession by hand, so at this point, you may wish to have the drum machine do it for you. Consult your Owner's Manual regarding song creation procedures for your machine. After you have done this, create a song titled *Verse1* with a *tempo of 115* and enter the previous four pattern sequence in the order shown. To make sure it sounds right, play it back.

It should be emphasized at this point that you cannot toss any old fill into your song. You must create fills that match and compliment your music. For this reason, when composing your first few songs it may be easier to program a fill first, then compose music around it.

Did you notice anything different when you keyed in Pattern 34? You should have noticed that the 1/4 Open Hi-hat was erased on numbers 9 and 13. Why was this? Well, in order for a drummer to strike the Snare and Toms with both sticks, he must remove his right stick from the Hi-hat. For this reason, the only possible sound to come from the Hi-hat during this motion is the pedal being stamped by his foot (the Hi-hat Pedal sound). In Pattern 34, I chose to leave it out. If you wish, you can place a Hi-hat Pedal on numbers 9, 11, 13, and 15. It will then look as Pattern 35. Either are perfectly fine and come down to personal preference.

Once again, this is so important that I'm going to repeat it. If it takes both sticks to hit the Toms or Snare, it is physically impossible to stick the Hi-hat during this motion.

Pattern 35 — Fill including Hi-hat Pedal

35	1st Measure																2nd Measure															
	1	2	3	4	5	6	7	8	9	10	11	12	13	14	15	16	1	2	3	4	5	6	7	8	9	10	11	12	13	14	15	16
Kick Bass	X		X			X	X			X		X					X		X			X		X		X	X			X			
Snare					X								X									X				X	X			X		X	X
Hi-hat Pedal																										X		X		X		X	
Closed Hi-hat																																	
1/4 Open Hi-hat		X	X	X		X	X	X			X	X	X	X	X		X					X											
Open Hi-hat	X				X				X				X																				
Ride (cup)																																	
Ride (edge)																																	
Tom 1																																	
Tom 2																																	
Tom 3																												X	X				
Tom 4																														X		X	

At this point, the lazy programmer would just repeat this 8 bar section twice to achieve a 16 bar Verse. As you might have guessed, we're not going to do that. We will now speed up the second half of our Verse by employing what we learned about Hi-hat rhythms in Chapter 3.

Exercise 10: To make the second half of our Verse sound faster, we will use a 1/16 note Hi-hat rhythm. This translates into a Hi-hat placed on every number between 1 and 16.

Looking back, the second measure of Pattern 29 uses a 1/4 note Hi-hat rhythm (a Hi-hat on every fourth number). This tends to slow the measure down. Notice that Pattern 20 from Chapter 3 is identical to Pattern 29 in all respects except, the Hi-hat in the second measure is comprised of 1/16 notes. Let's use Pattern 20 as the basic rhythm pattern for the second half of the Verse.

At this point, for reasons discussed earlier, we will need a Rhythm fill for the end of the 12th measure. In the same manner as before, either copy Pattern 20 to 36 and modify it to look as follows, or punch it in from scratch.

Pattern 36 — Rhythm Fill

36	1st Measure																2nd Measure															
	1	2	3	4	5	6	7	8	9	10	11	12	13	14	15	16	1	2	3	4	5	6	7	8	9	10	11	12	13	14	15	16
KickBass	X	X			X	X		X		X										X	X			X	X		X		X			X
Snare					X								X									X								X		
Hi-hat Pedal																																
Closed Hi-hat																																
1/4 Open Hi-hat		X	X	X		X	X	X		X	X	X	X				X	X	X	X		X	X							X	X	X	X
Open Hi-hat	X				X			X					X								X		X		X		X					
Ride (cup)																																
Ride (edge)																																
Tom 1																																
Tom 2																																
Tom 3																																
Tom 4																																

Pattern 36 has a first measure identical to that of Pattern 20. However, in the second measure, the Kick and Hi-hat rhythms are different. This is exactly what is meant by a Rhythm Fill.

EARLY MUSIC SYNTHESIZER

Exercise 11: To finish the Verse, let's use a Snare and Tom Fill at the end of the 16th measure. This time, let's make it a full bar.

Pattern 37 contains the 1 bar fill we're looking for. Either copy Pattern 20 to 37 then delete and add notes, or punch it in from scratch.

Pattern 37 — 1 Bar Fill

37	1st Measure																2nd Measure															
	1	2	3	4	5	6	7	8	9	10	11	12	13	14	15	16	1	2	3	4	5	6	7	8	9	10	11	12	13	14	15	16
KickBass	X		X			X	X		X			X			X		X		X		X		X	X		X			X			
Snare				X									X				X	X					X					X				
Hi-hat Pedal																	X		X		X		X		X		X		X		X	
Closed Hi-hat																																
1/4 Open Hi-hat		X	X	X		X	X	X		X	X	X	X	X																		
Open Hi-hat	X				X				X						X																	
Ride (cup)																																
Ride (edge)																																
Tom 1																					X	X										
Tom 2																							X	X		X						
Tom 3																									X	X		X	X			
Tom 4																											X		X		X	X

Let's generalize 5 things about Pattern 37.

1) ***The Toms are generally played in numerical order from highest pitched (Tom 1) to lowest (Tom 4).*** For example, if you start a fill with Tom 2 and have no idea which Tom to hit next, a good choice would be Tom 3, and then Tom 4. *(Keep in mind that some drum machines use an opposite convention where Tom 1 is the lowest pitched. If you are affected, flip this generalization around.)*

2) Upon more analysis, you will notice that the fill started with two stickings of the Snare, followed by two stickings of Tom 1, two Tom 2's, two Tom 3's, and ended on Tom 4, thus taking a symmetric and numerical path. **Two is indeed a magical number in 1/16 quantization** because the aforementioned method is a common way to break into a Tom fill.

3) Also notice that **at no time does it take more than two hands or feet to play this pattern.** When programming, it may help you to put it in tabulature form to see how many limbs it will take. Flip to the end of this text for blank tabulature sheets.

4) As for the Hi-hat motion, **the only humanly possible sound emanating from the Hi-hat during the Tom fill was the Hi-hat Pedal.** It can be placed at 2 number intervals (1/8 note Hi-hat rhythm), or any spacing you wish. Experiment with the Hi-hat Pedal and determine what sounds best to you.

5) **Note that it is humanly possible to hit the Snare and a Tom at the same time. It is also possible to hit two Toms at the same time.** Both of these are standard practice for a real drummer and should be incorporated into your drumming technique as in Pattern 37.

In Exercise 13 we will construct an 8 bar Chorus. It will be different from the Verse in the respect that it will use 1/32 quantization in conjunction with one of the fills. If you've ever wondered how to get faster sticking into your fills without increasing the tempo of your drum machine, this is it.

Exercise 12: If you haven't done so already, now is the time to consult your Owner's Manual regarding song creation. Although you can play the following pattern sequence by hand, you'll save your fingers some trouble if you let the machine do it for you. Create a song, call it *Verse1*, use a tempo of 115, and place the following patterns in sequence under it.

Verse 1
Pattern 29
Pattern 33
Pattern 29
Pattern 34
Pattern 20
Pattern 36
Pattern 20
Pattern 37

Tell me it's nice.

Exercise 13: And now for the Chorus. Let's keep it short and sweet and limit it to 8 bars. Keep in mind that a Chorus can be as long as you wish, however 8 bars is the most common length. As mentioned in Chapter 3, we would either like to use the Open Hi-hat or Ride cymbal in the Chorus. Pattern 31 from Chapter 3 will be a good choice for the basic drum rhythm since it meets this criteria.

We do not wish to repeat Pattern 31 four times for a total of 8 bars. Just as before, we will place a fill at the end of every fourth measure. We could use a Rhythm Fill as before, but for the sake of practice, let's make it a 1/2 bar Snare and Tom Fill.

Copy Pattern 31 to Pattern 38. Using the usual techniques, make your Pattern 38 identical to the following utilizing Step Mode.

Pattern 38   1/2 Bar Fill

38	1st Measure																2nd Measure															
	1	2	3	4	5	6	7	8	9	10	11	12	13	14	15	16	1	2	3	4	5	6	7	8	9	10	11	12	13	14	15	16
Kick Bass	X		X	X			X				X								X				X	X	X		X		X		X	
Snare					X							X									X			X					X	X	X	
Hi-hat Pedal																																	
Closed Hi-hat																																	
1/4 Open Hi-hat																																	
Open Hi-hat																																	
Ride (cup)	X		X		X		X		X		X		X		X		X		X		X		X	X		X						
Ride (edge)																																	
Tom 1																																	
Tom 2																																	
Tom 3																																	
Tom 4																																	

Now listen to Patterns 31 and 38 in succession.

Playing With Quantization

For simplicity sake, when starting this text it was my intention to do all programming in 1/16 quantization. After reaching this chapter however, I feel I must briefly expose you to programming in another quantization. Honestly, it is not that difficult. 1/32 quantization is much like 1/16 quantization, the only difference is that instead of 16, each measure is divided into 32 pieces.

Exercise 14: Let's compose the final fill for our Chorus. Again, as with the final fill of the Verse, we will make it one bar long. Copy Pattern 31 to Pattern 39. Notice this time that the following tabulature is in 1/32 quantization. Your machine does not have to be in 1/32 quantization to copy the pattern, however, you will need to change it if you wish to edit the pattern in Step Mode. If you are unsure how to change the quantization of your machine, consult your Owner's Manual (It is usually a very simple operation that involves pushing only 1 or 2 buttons). When you have changed the quantization, enter the following pattern into your drum machine using your usual methods.

If you find it confusing to work in 1/32 quantization, refer back to Table 1 in the Quantization section of Chapter 1 for guidance. There you will find a correlation between 1/16 quantization and 1/32 quantization; The 1/16 quantization numbers are simply the odds of 1/32. Most every note of Pattern 39 occurs on an odd number. This implies that the majority of the programming could therefore be done in 1/16 quantization. This is correct. However, you would eventually have to change your machine to 1/32 quantization in order to program the notes appearing on the even numbers 4 and 12. For the sake of argument, if you were to go 180 degrees in the other direction and change your machine to 1/96 quantization, notice (looking at Table 1 in Chapter 1) that Pattern 39 could be entered in its entirety since every space in 1/32 quantization exists in 1/96 quantization. You may wish to do this as a practice exercise at your own leisure.

Pattern 39

39 — 1st Measure

	1	2	3	4	5	6	7	8	9	10	11	12	13	14	15	16	17	18	19	20	21	22	23	24	25	26	27	28	29	30	31	32
Kick Bass	X				X	X							X								X											
Snare									X																X							
Hi-hat Pedal																																
Closed Hi-hat																																
1/4 Open Hi-hat																																
Open Hi-hat																																
Ride (cup)	X				X				X				X				X				X				X				X			
Ride (edge)																																
Tom 1																																
Tom 2																																
Tom 3																																
Tom 4																																

The second measure of Pattern 39 appears on the following page

One Bar Fill

39 — 2nd Measure

	1	2	3	4	5	6	7	8	9	10	11	12	13	14	15	16	17	18	19	20	21	22	23	24	25	26	27	28	29	30	31	32
Kick Bass	X			X			X			X			X				X				X	X						X				
Snare	X		X	X	X																				X							
Hi-hat Pedal																																
Closed Hi-hat																																
1/4 Open Hi-hat																																
Open Hi-hat																																
Ride (cup)																																
Ride (edge)																																
Tom 1									X		X	X	X																			
Tom 2																		X		X												
Tom 3																					X											
Tom 4																									X		X		X			

Notice that Snare notes appear on numbers 3, 4, and 5 of the second measure. Also notice that Tom notes appear on numbers 11, 12, and 13. The speed you hear in the fill is due to the "three in a row" architecture (one even in between two odd). In 1/32 quantization, these spurts of three in a row will add the speed you are looking for.

Exercise 15: Let's take a listen to the complete Chorus. Play the following patterns in succession.

Chorus
Pattern **31**
Pattern **38**
Pattern **31**
Pattern **39**

That's it. It's that simple to compose either a Chorus or Verse. The only tough part is coming up with the fills to match your music. With a little practice, even that will be easy.

Again, here are 2 helpful rules to follow until you acquire your own fill technique.

1) *Play the Toms in increasing numerical order (Tom1 to Tom4) with the ultimate goal being to get to Tom 4 (the floor tom) by the end of the fill.*

2) *If the sticking in your fills isn't happening fast enough, change to 1/32 quantization and place your notes on three numbers in a row (two odds and an even). Placement as such will bring faster sticking without increasing the tempo of your drum machine.*

I would like to explain the difference between 1/32 and 1/16 quantization once again for clarity. As you can imagine, with 32 pieces, there are 16 that will not appear if you change your machine back to 1/16 quantization. The pattern will sound the same, however the difference will occur when you enter Step Mode. Here, you will see only 16 of the original 32 pieces. They are: 1, 3, 5, 7, 9, 13, 15, 17, 19, 21, 23, 25, 27, 29, and 31. Yes, all of the odd numbers. You won't be able to see any notes that were on even numbers, yet the drum machine knows that they are there and they will be heard when the pattern is played.

On a similar note, if you enter a rhythm into your drum machine using the Real Time Mode, then enter Step Mode, you may not be able to see all of the notes that you punched in. This is because some Real Time Modes use a quantization of 1/96 and beyond to record your motions. If you are stepping through a pattern that was recorded using 1/96 quantization and you are now in 1/16 quantization, there are 80 (96 - 16 = 80) numbers that you won't be able to see unless you change your machine back to 1/96 quantization. The notes are there, all you have to do is change the quantization to see them.

In Chapter 1, I mentioned that there was another way to flam if your drum machine did not have a flam button. It can be easily accomplished by placing your machine in a small quantization then putting two Snares on numbers adjacent to one another. For example, place your machine in 1/96 quantization then put a Snare on numbers 73 and 74. Now play the pattern back at tempo of 100. What you hear is what is known as a flam. As mentioned in Chapter 1, a flam entails striking a drum head with both sticks, a split second apart. The problem with this method is two fold. First, the speed of the flam is now a function of the tempo. If you increase the tempo to say 250, the two Snare notes will sound as one. How do you get around this? Place the Snare notes at a wider interval. For example, 73 and 75. Second, when producing a flam, a real drummer will strike the drum head using less force with one stick. To solve this dilemma you will need to decrease the volume of one of the notes slightly. If you have a newer drum machine, this can be done in the *edit pattern mode*. This mode will allow you to edit the parameters of any single note in a programmed pattern. Or, if your machine has touch sensitive pads, simply hit the pad softer on one note.

As you've seen in this chapter, Tom-toms are an integral part of drumming. They are mainly used for fills but can also be incorporated into a basic drum rhythm. Use them and experiment!

-Chapter 5-

More Cymbals

The Crash, China, and Splash

The preceding four chapters have provided many helpful hints to make your drum programming sound more realistic. There are yet a few more suggestions which we will discuss in this fifth and final chapter.

The last pieces of drum hardware to be covered are the Crash, China, and Splash cymbals. *(Note that the Hi-hat and Ride are also cymbals, but because of the similar sticking techniques used to strike them, they were grouped together and covered in Chapter 2).* If your drum programming is still lacking the realism you desire, the Crash, China, and Splash cymbals will provide it. In addition, they will also provide a means to create a wider tonal variation in your music. On that note, many programmers fail to use cymbals and it shows in the tedium of their songs. A good analogy for this type of programming might be listening to a monotonic public speaker. After ten minutes you're drowsy, and after twenty you're comatose. Some drum programming makes me feel this way. On the other hand, other programmers use cymbals, but fail to climax their music effectively. To avoid these pitfalls, use the three rules of thumb that will be mentioned later in this chapter, and above all, experiment! Experimentation will lead to cymbal placements that sound best with your music. Let's take a closer look at what makes each of these cymbals sound unique.

The **Crash**, as with all cymbals, comes in assorted thicknesses and diameters, each resonating at a different pitch. Its basic shape is always the same and resembles that of an upside-down saucer. If you have ever heard a marching band leader crash two cymbals together, then you are already familiar with the bright tone that this cymbal makes.

The **China** is much the same size as the Crash, but differs in thickness, shape, and tone. When looking at one, you will notice that the outer edge spoon up. It is this shape in conjunction with its thin construction that produces its characteristic dull tone.

The **Splash** is essentially a mini Crash. Because of its small diameter it resonates at a higher pitch than either of the previously mentioned two. Unfortunately, since it does not come as a stock sample in most drum machines it will not be used in this chapter. The main reason you would want to use one is for the same reasons stated before. Since it is struck in much the same manner as the Crash and China, should you ever obtain a Splash sample in the future, the information contained in this chapter should be an adequate guide for its placement in your programming.

Most drum machines contain very few cymbal samples. A China sample will occasionally be found, but few contain a Splash. The only sample resident in most drum machines is the Crash. Even though newer machines have made headway in this area with much more numerous samples than previous models, there are still relatively few (comparatively speaking to what you would find in a good sized real kit).

Most real drummers have a large array of different diameter Crash cymbals in their kit. This makes it possible to match the pitch of the cymbal with the sound of the music. Most newer drum machines will similarly allow the user to vary the pitch of the samples. This works to a certain degree, but becomes terribly unrealistic as pitch variations become extreme (and sometimes even when not so extreme).

Keep in mind that it will require experimentation to place cymbals where they sound best in your music. To shorten the learning curve, I suggest that you take a stroll down to your local nightclub and watch a real drummer in action. Take special note of how he/she will accent notes and chordes with cymbal Crashes. Also note the way he/she will use a cymbal to crescendo a section of music. Keep in mind that even an oddly placed cymbal can add a new twist to your music. In the case of cymbals, a picture will certainly be worth a thousand words. Even if your television is as close as you can get to a real drummer, a few hours of MTV will help.

As with any other piece of drum hardware, the cymbals have certain regularities of use. Here are 3 rules of thumb.

1) *A Crash cymbal is almost always accompanied by an accented kick of the bass drum.* Even though it is your prerogative to place Kicks anywhere you wish, I think you will find that it sounds best when you do this.

2) *A Crash cymbal on the first number of the first measure of every Verse and Chorus is pretty standard.* Generally more are used, but this is a good starting point.

3) *A Crash cymbal is almost always placed on the first number of the measure immediately following a fill.*

If you're confused, hang tight, these three rules will be exemplified throughout the chapter.

Intro's, Bridges, and Finalés

Intro's, Bridges, and Finalés are very important pieces of your song. They are responsible for making the transitions between Verse and Chorus, Chorus and Verse, and beginning and end, sound smooth. Without them, your song might seem mechanical, boring, and unrefined. Even though it is important to have a good Verse and Chorus, without these three pieces, your song may not be the best it can possibly be. The length of your Intro, Bridge, or Finale can be 1, 2, or more measures long and involve just about any sounds you wish. The only catch is that they must create a smooth transition from one part to the next.

The Intro

We've all heard an Intro before. It can involve just about anything. The bottom line is that it must ease the listener into the song. I have basically 3 favorites: four counts on the Hi-hat, a one or two measure fill, and an 8 or 16 bar combinational drum and guitar lead-in. Pattern 40 contains a two measure fill that we will use as the Intro to our song.

Exercise 16: Let's add a 2 measure Intro (introductory phrase) to our song. Enter Pattern 40 into your drum machine as follows.

Pattern 40   Intro

40	1st Measure																2nd Measure															
	1	2	3	4	5	6	7	8	9	10	11	12	13	14	15	16	1	2	3	4	5	6	7	8	9	10	11	12	13	14	15	16
Kick Bass	A	X	X		X		A		A		A						X		X	X		A		X	A		A					
Snare				X							X										X				X		X	X	X			
Hi-hat Pedal																																
Closed Hi-hat																																
1/4 Open Hi-hat			X	X			X	X		X							X		X	X												
Open Hi-hat					X																	X										
Ride (cup)																																
Ride (edge)																																
Tom 1																																
Tom 2																																
Tom 3																																
Tom 4																																
Crash	X						X			X												X							X			
China													X									X										

I'm sure you've noticed that for the first time there were cymbals in the pattern. Why were they placed where they were? Well, cymbals are something that you just have to place by ear, instinct, and the three rules of thumb mentioned earlier in this chapter. Notice that each Crash and China cymbal is accented with a kick of the bass drum (Rule #1). As mentioned earlier, this is a common technique. Let's do a few more examples and see if we can shine more light on cymbal use.

The Bridge

A good Bridge will fuse two sections of a song such that there are no rough edges and the transition is smooth. Like an Intro, a Bridge can vary greatly in size and sound. Good Bridges are hard to spot because they are often mistaken as part of the Verse or Chorus. If your Verse and Chorus flow smoothly into each other, then you probably don't need one. On the other hand, if you have a vocal section that doesn't belong in the Verse or Chorus, you might consider using one to accommodate the additional words. A Bridge can also be used to give breathing room between the Chorus and Verse or vice-versa.

Next, a one measure Bridge will be used to fuse the end of our Chorus with the beginning of the Verse.

Exercise 17: A Bridge is quite easy to fabricate after a little practice, especially if it's only 1 measure. Enter Pattern 41 into your drum machine.

Pattern 41   Bridge

41	1st Measure															
	1	2	3	4	5	6	7	8	9	10	11	12	13	14	15	16
KickBass	X		A		X		X		A		X				A	
Snare	X	X					X	X					X			
Hi-hat Pedal																
Closed Hi-hat																
1/4 Open Hi-hat																
Open Hi-hat																
Ride (cup)																
Ride (edge)																
Tom 1																
Tom 2																
Tom 3					X											
Tom 4	X						X				X					
Crash			X						X						X	
China																

The Finalé

A Finalé, just as an Intro or Bridge, can be just about as long as you want as long as the song doesn't suffer from its use. I usually keep it short and sweet (less than 8 bars). It too can involve just about any sounds you wish, as long as it does its job, which is, to ease the listener out of the song and leave him/her with a strong sense that it's over.

Composing a Finalé for your song can be quite tricky and sound quite phony with a drum machine if you are not selective about how you do it. For example, it is difficult to create a good crescendo or decrescendo using the cymbal samples in most drum machines. Therefore, unless you have a sample of a crescendo or decrescendo it is basically out of the question. There are still many ways to end a song. One such way will be shown in the next exercise.

Exercise 18: The following is a 2 bar Finalé that should be entered into your drum machine as Pattern 42. It is short and sweet and most often the best way to end a song if you are using a drum machine.

Pattern 42 — Finalé

42

	1st Measure																2nd Measure															
	1	2	3	4	5	6	7	8	9	10	11	12	13	14	15	16	1	2	3	4	5	6	7	8	9	10	11	12	13	14	15	16
Kick Bass			X		X				X		X						A															
Snare	X						X						X																			
Hi-hat Pedal																																
Closed Hi-hat																																
1/4 Open Hi-hat																																
Open Hi-hat																																
Ride (cup)																																
Ride (edge)																																
Tom 1																																
Tom 2																																
Tom 3																																
Tom 4	X					X					X																					
Crash																	X															
China																																

Putting It All Together

SONG 1
Structure D

At this point, we are ready to put our song together. Keep in mind that we still need to add cymbals to the Verse and Chorus, but by using the three rules stated earlier in this chapter, that should not be a problem. Our song is *Structure D* type as outlined in Chapter 1 with song components as follow.

Using this table, *Song 1 (outlined as Structure D)* can be entered as a sequence of patterns into your drum machine memory. This will turn out to be a sequence of 49 patterns as you can see from the table. Consult your Owner's Manual for directions on song creation if you are not already sure how it's done. Choose a **tempo of 115** and a **time of 4/4** for Song 1.

Intro	40
Chorus (no vocals)	31
	38
	31
	39
Verse #1 (vocals)	29
	33
	29
	34
	20
	36
	20
	37
Bridge	41
Chorus (vocals)	31
	38
	31
	39
Verse #2 (vocals)	29
	33
	29
	34
	20
	36
	20
	37
Bridge	41
Chorus (vocals)	31
	38
	31
	39
Verse (solo)	29
	33
	29
	34
	20
	36
	20
	37
Bridge	41
Chorus (vocals)	31
	38
	31
	39
Chorus (vocals)	31
	38
	31
	39
Finalé	42

Exercise 19: In order to add cymbals to the Verse and Chorus, let's apply the three rules stated earlier in this chapter.

1) *A cymbal Crash is almost always accompanied by an accented kick of the bass drum.* Even though it is your prerogative to place Kicks anywhere you wish, I think you will find that it sounds best when you do this.
2) *A cymbal Crash on the first number of the first measure of every Verse and Chorus is pretty standard.* Generally more are used, but this is a good starting point.
3) *A cymbal Crash is almost always placed on the first number of the measure immediately following a fill.*

Applying these rules to our song, we will place a cymbal Crash on the first number of the first measure of the Verse and Chorus (Rule #2). Second, we will place an accented Kick wherever a cymbal Crash occurs (Rule #1). And third, we will place a cymbal Crash on the first number of the measure immediately following a fill (Rule #3).

Applying Rules #2 and #3, Patterns 29 and 20 of the Verse need a Crash on number 1. Pattern 31 of the Chorus also needs the same. This implies that we need to exercise Rule #2 which is to accent the Kick wherever a cymbal Crash occurs. The tabulature for these improvements appears on the following three pages, all you need to do is enter Step Mode and make the listed changes. *Sometimes the Hi-hat is removed when it is physically impossible to play, or when it just doesn't sound good.* Make the changes, then listen to the final product.

Pattern 20 — *No* Cymbals

20	1st Measure																2nd Measure															
	1	2	3	4	5	6	7	8	9	10	11	12	13	14	15	16	1	2	3	4	5	6	7	8	9	10	11	12	13	14	15	16
Kick Bass	X	X			X		X			X			X				X		X			X		X		X						X
Snare					X								X								X								X			
Hi-hat Pedal																																
Closed Hi-hat																																
1/4 Open Hi-hat		X	X	X		X	X	X		X	X	X	X	X		X	X	X	X		X	X	X		X		X	X	X	X
Open Hi-hat	X				X				X				X					X				X			X						X

Pattern 20 — With Cymbals

20	1st Measure																2nd Measure															
	1	2	3	4	5	6	7	8	9	10	11	12	13	14	15	16	1	2	3	4	5	6	7	8	9	10	11	12	13	14	15	16
Kick Bass	A	X			X		X			X			X				X		X			X		X		X						X
Snare					X								X								X								X			
Hi-hat Pedal																																
Closed Hi-hat																																
1/4 Open Hi-hat			X	X		X	X	X		X	X	X	X	X		X	X	X	X		X	X	X		X		X	X	X	X
Open Hi-hat					X				X				X					X				X		X						X
Ride (cup)																																
Ride (edge)																																
Tom 1																																
Tom 2																																
Tom 3																																
Tom 4																																
Crash	X																															
China																																

Pattern 29 — No Cymbals

29	1st Measure																	2nd Measure															
	1	2	3	4	5	6	7	8	9	10	11	12	13	14	15	16	1	2	3	4	5	6	7	8	9	10	11	12	13	14	15	16
Kick Bass	X		X			X	X		X			X			X		X		X			X		X	X						X	
Snare					X								X								X									X		
Hi-hat Pedal																																
Closed Hi-hat																																
1/4 Open Hi-hat		X	X	X		X	X	X		X	X	X	X	X			X				X				X				X			
Open Hi-hat	X				X				X						X																	

Pattern 29 — With Cymbals

29	1st Measure																	2nd Measure															
	1	2	3	4	5	6	7	8	9	10	11	12	13	14	15	16	1	2	3	4	5	6	7	8	9	10	11	12	13	14	15	16
Kick Bass	A		X			X			X			X			X		X		X			X		X	X						X	
Snare					X								X								X									X		
Hi-hat Pedal																																
Closed Hi-hat																																
1/4 Open Hi-hat			X	X		X	X	X		X	X	X	X	X			X				X				X				X			
Open Hi-hat					X				X						X																	
Ride (cup)																																
Ride (edge)																																
Tom 1																																
Tom 2																																
Tom 3																																
Tom 4																																
Crash	X																															
China																																

Pattern 31 — *No* Cymbals

31 — 1st Measure / 2nd Measure

	1	2	3	4	5	6	7	8	9	10	11	12	13	14	15	16	1	2	3	4	5	6	7	8	9	10	11	12	13	14	15	16
Kick Bass	X		X	X			X				X								X				X			X	X				X	
Snare					X							X									X								X			
Hi-hat Pedal																																
Closed Hi-hat																																
1/4 Open Hi-hat																																
Open Hi-hat																																
Ride (cup)	X		X		X		X		X		X		X		X		X		X		X		X		X		X		X		X	
Ride (edge)																																

Pattern 31 — With Cymbals

31 — 1st Measure / 2nd Measure

	1	2	3	4	5	6	7	8	9	10	11	12	13	14	15	16	1	2	3	4	5	6	7	8	9	10	11	12	13	14	15	16
Kick Bass	A		X	X			X				X								X				X			X	X				X	
Snare					X							X									X								X			
Hi-hat Pedal																																
Closed Hi-hat																																
1/4 Open Hi-hat																																
Open Hi-hat																																
Ride (cup)			X		X		X		X		X		X		X		X		X		X		X		X		X		X		X	
Ride (edge)																																
Tom 1																																
Tom 2																																
Tom 3																																
Tom 4																																
Crash	X																															
China																																

Inclusion of cymbals in the preceding patterns added expression and improved realism tremendously. As with all programming though, you will wish to fine tune the cymbal notes. For example, experiment with pitch and volume changes. Selectively increase and decrease cymbal volume and pitch to produce a wider range in tonality. As mentioned earlier, depending on the age of your machine you may be limited in this area. Experiment, but above all, don't forget to use the cymbals!

LET'S RECAP THE THOUGHT PROCESS USED TO CREATE A DRUM TRACK

1. Lay down a 2 bar Kick and Snare rhythm that compliments your guitar riff, keyboard melody, bass line, etc. As shown in Chapter 2, the Snare always goes on numbers 5 and 13 when in 1/16 quantization. For Rap rhythms, try adding a Snare on 8 and/or 10 in addition to 5 and 13.

2. (A) After completing Step 1, copy the Kick and Snare rhythm to a few empty patterns and add 1/4, 1/8, and 1/16 note Hi-hat rhythms as described in Chapter 3. Try using different Hi-hat samples in the patterns. Your ultimate goal should be to find a rhythm that sounds best with your music. Use the guidelines presented in Chapter 3 and experiment. For Rap rhythms, try adding a Tambourine or Shaker on the numbers 1, 3, 4, 5, 7, 8, 9, 11, 12, 13, and 15.

   (B) Once again, copy the Kick and Snare rhythm to a few more empty patterns. This time, add different Ride cymbal rhythms.

   (C) Compare all of the patterns created in Steps 2A and 2B and determine which *one* sounds the best with your music. This is the pattern that you will use as the basis for your Verse or Chorus. The question is, how do you decide which to use it in? Consult the section of this text entitled *Which Do I Choose?* It is located in Chapter 3 and will provide some guidelines for making this decision.

3. (A) Copy the pattern chosen in Step 2C to a few empty patterns. This time, add different Rhythm Fills as described in Chapter 4. Recall that a Rhythm Fill is a change in the Kick and/or Hi-hat rhythm at or near the end of a measure. As before, decide on a favorite.

   (B) Once again, copy the pattern chosen in Step 2C to a few more empty patterns. This time, create large and small fills using whatever sounds you wish. The techniques shown in Chapter 4 will be quite applicable here, just remember to remove the Hi-hat and Ride cymbal notes where they are physically impossible for a real drummer to play. Note that the number of fills you will need to create depends on the length of your Verse or Chorus and what sounds best to you. Generally, the length of a Chorus or Verse will be a multiple of 8 bars. More specifically, a 16 bar Verse and an 8 bar Chorus are quite common. In a 16 bar Verse you may wish to place Rhythm Fills at the end of the 4th and 12th measures, a large fill at the end of the 16th, and a small fill at the end of the 8th. Determine which fills sound best with your music, and as shown in Chapter 4, construct your Verse or Chorus.

4. If you have just completed the drumming for your Verse, repeat Steps 1 through 3 to compose the Chorus. Likewise, if you have just composed the Chorus, compose the Verse.

5. If you haven't done so already, now is the time to determine a structure for your song. For a few examples, consult the section in Chapter 1 entitled *Song Structures*. Try a few different arrangements to see how your song sounds best. This will require creating an Intro, and depending upon your structure, may also require a Bridge and Finalé. Consult Chapter 5 for instruction on creating these sections.

6. You are now ready to add the Crash, China, and Splash cymbals as described in Chapter 5. Follow the three rules of thumb stated there and once again, remove the Hi-hat and Ride cymbal notes where they are physically impossible to play.

7. **SAVE YOUR WORK!**

Composing a drum track is that simple and will become second nature after you have done it a few times.

Hang in there!

Congratulations! You have now completed this text and will be producing great sounding drum rhythms in no time. As you have just learned, the rudiments of drumming are not that difficult. Your real challenge lays in learning the keystrokes to operate your machine. With the exercises presented herein, you now have a good foundation from which to build your drumming technique. Take what you have just learned and experiment. Break the rules! Use the aforementioned guidelines merely as a starting point, and fall back on them only in times of indecision. It is in this manner that you will develop a style all your own and excel over the creations of others. If you do not intend to have a real drummer play your rhythms, then the sky is the limit, and indeed you should try sampling it!

Blank Drum Machine Tabulature

	1st Measure																2nd Measure															
	1	2	3	4	5	6	7	8	9	10	11	12	13	14	15	16	1	2	3	4	5	6	7	8	9	10	11	12	13	14	15	16
Kick Bass																																	
Snare																																	
Hi-hat Pedal																																	
Closed Hi-hat																																	
1/4 Open Hi-hat																																	
Open Hi-hat																																	
Ride edge																																	
Ride cup																																	
Tom 1																																	
Tom 2																																	
Tom 3																																	
Tom 4																																	
Crash																																	
China																																	

	1st Measure																2nd Measure															
	1	2	3	4	5	6	7	8	9	10	11	12	13	14	15	16	1	2	3	4	5	6	7	8	9	10	11	12	13	14	15	16
Kick Bass																																	
Snare																																	
Hi-hat Pedal																																	
Closed Hi-hat																																	
1/4 Open Hi-hat																																	
Open Hi-hat																																	
Ride edge																																	
Ride cup																																	
Tom 1																																	
Tom 2																																	
Tom 3																																	
Tom 4																																	
Crash																																	
China																																	

	1st Measure																2nd Measure															
	1	2	3	4	5	6	7	8	9	10	11	12	13	14	15	16	1	2	3	4	5	6	7	8	9	10	11	12	13	14	15	16
Kick Bass																																
Snare																																
Hi-hat Pedal																																
Closed Hi-hat																																
1/4 Open Hi-hat																																
Open Hi-hat																																
Ride edge																																
Ride cup																																
Tom 1																																
Tom 2																																
Tom 3																																
Tom 4																																
Crash																																
China																																

	1st Measure																2nd Measure															
	1	2	3	4	5	6	7	8	9	10	11	12	13	14	15	16	1	2	3	4	5	6	7	8	9	10	11	12	13	14	15	16
Kick Bass																																
Snare																																
Hi-hat Pedal																																
Closed Hi-hat																																
1/4 Open Hi-hat																																
Open Hi-hat																																
Ride edge																																
Ride cup																																
Tom 1																																
Tom 2																																
Tom 3																																
Tom 4																																
Crash																																
China																																

	1st Measure																2nd Measure															
	1	2	3	4	5	6	7	8	9	10	11	12	13	14	15	16	1	2	3	4	5	6	7	8	9	10	11	12	13	14	15	16
Kick Bass																																
Snare																																
Hi-hat Pedal																																
Closed Hi-hat																																
1/4 Open Hi-hat																																
Open Hi-hat																																
Ride edge																																
Ride cup																																
Tom 1																																
Tom 2																																
Tom 3																																
Tom 4																																
Crash																																
China																																

	1st Measure																2nd Measure															
	1	2	3	4	5	6	7	8	9	10	11	12	13	14	15	16	1	2	3	4	5	6	7	8	9	10	11	12	13	14	15	16
Kick Bass																																
Snare																																
Hi-hat Pedal																																
Closed Hi-hat																																
1/4 Open Hi-hat																																
Open Hi-hat																																
Ride edge																																
Ride cup																																
Tom 1																																
Tom 2																																
Tom 3																																
Tom 4																																
Crash																																
China																																

	1st Measure																2nd Measure															
	1	2	3	4	5	6	7	8	9	10	11	12	13	14	15	16	1	2	3	4	5	6	7	8	9	10	11	12	13	14	15	16

	1st Measure																2nd Measure															
	1	2	3	4	5	6	7	8	9	10	11	12	13	14	15	16	1	2	3	4	5	6	7	8	9	10	11	12	13	14	15	16

	1st Measure																2nd Measure															
	1	2	3	4	5	6	7	8	9	10	11	12	13	14	15	16	1	2	3	4	5	6	7	8	9	10	11	12	13	14	15	16

	1st Measure																2nd Measure															
	1	2	3	4	5	6	7	8	9	10	11	12	13	14	15	16	1	2	3	4	5	6	7	8	9	10	11	12	13	14	15	16

	1st Measure																2nd Measure															
	1	2	3	4	5	6	7	8	9	10	11	12	13	14	15	16	1	2	3	4	5	6	7	8	9	10	11	12	13	14	15	16

	1st Measure																2nd Measure															
	1	2	3	4	5	6	7	8	9	10	11	12	13	14	15	16	1	2	3	4	5	6	7	8	9	10	11	12	13	14	15	16

	1st Measure																2nd Measure															
	1	2	3	4	5	6	7	8	9	10	11	12	13	14	15	16	1	2	3	4	5	6	7	8	9	10	11	12	13	14	15	16

	1st Measure																2nd Measure															
	1	2	3	4	5	6	7	8	9	10	11	12	13	14	15	16	1	2	3	4	5	6	7	8	9	10	11	12	13	14	15	16

	1st Measure																2nd Measure															
	1	2	3	4	5	6	7	8	9	10	11	12	13	14	15	16	1	2	3	4	5	6	7	8	9	10	11	12	13	14	15	16

	1st Measure																2nd Measure															
	1	2	3	4	5	6	7	8	9	10	11	12	13	14	15	16	1	2	3	4	5	6	7	8	9	10	11	12	13	14	15	16

	1st Measure																2nd Measure															
	1	2	3	4	5	6	7	8	9	10	11	12	13	14	15	16	1	2	3	4	5	6	7	8	9	10	11	12	13	14	15	16

	1st Measure																2nd Measure															
	1	2	3	4	5	6	7	8	9	10	11	12	13	14	15	16	1	2	3	4	5	6	7	8	9	10	11	12	13	14	15	16

You'll Like What You Hear!

Guitar books from Centerstream Publishing
P.O. Box 17878 - Anaheim Hills, CA 92807 (714) - 779-9390

Guitar Chords Plus
by Ron Middlebrook
Centerstream Publishing
A comprehensive study of normal and extended chords, tuning, keys, transposing, capo, and more. Includes lots of helpful photos and diagrams, a key to guitar symbols, and a glossary of guitar terms.
00000011 ....$11.95

Pedal Steel Licks For Guitar*
by Forest Rodgers
Centerstream Publishing
Learn to play 30 popular pedal steel licks on the guitar. All 30 examples are played three times on the accompanying CD. Also features tips for the best steel guitar sound reproduction, and steel guitar voiced chords.
_____00000183 Book/CD Pack $15.95

Electric Blues Guitar
by Derek Cornett
Centerstream Publications
An introduction to the most commonly used scales and techniques for the modern blues player, complete with CD. Includes musical examples to show how scales are used in improvisation, and play-along tunes that provide a "hands-on" start to improvisation.
_____00000165 Book/CD Pack........................$17.95

Blues Guitar Legends
by Kenny Sultan
Centerstream Publishing
This book/CD package allows you to explore the styles of Lightnin' Hopkins, Blind Blake, Mississippi John Hurt, Blind Boy Fuller, and Big Bill Broonzy. Through Sultan's arrangements, you will learn how studying the masters can help you develop your own style.
_____00000181 Book/CD Pack $19.95

SCALES AND MODES IN THE BEGINNING
by Ron Middlebrook
Centerstream Publications
The most comprehensive and complete scale book written especially for the guitar. Divided into four main sections: 1) Fretboard Visualization, the breaking down of the whole into parts; 2) Scale Terminology – a thorough understanding of whole and half steps, scale degrees, intervals, etc.; 3) Scales And Modes – the rear of the book covers every scale you will ever need with exercises and applications; 4) Scale To Chord Guide – ties it all together, showing what scale to use over various chords.
_____00000010............................$11.95

POWER RHYTHM GUITAR
by Ron Middlebrook with Dave Celentano
Centerstream Publications
This book/CD pack features 31 lessons for rhythm guitar that you can play by yourself, in a band, or as a back-up musician. Includes full band examples in many musical styles, including basic rock, country, hard rock, heavy metal, reggae, blues, funk, and more.
_____00000113 Book/CD Pack...................$17.95

Flying Fingers*
by Dave Celentano
Centerstream Publications
Your fingers will be flying over the guitar neck as this book/cassette demonstrates proven techniques that increase speed, precision and dexterity. 32 examples cover alternate picking, sweep picking and circular picking. Cassette demonstrates techniques at three speeds: slow, medium and fast.
_____00000103 Book/Cassette Pack............$15.95

Modal Jams And Theory
Using The Modes For Solo Guitar
by Dave Celentano
Centerstream Publications
Not only will this book show you how to play the modes, it will also show you the theory behind mode construction, how to play any mode in any key, how to play the proper mode over a given chord progression, and how to write chord progressions for each of the seven modes. The accompanying CD includes two rhythm tracks (drums, bass, keyboard and rhythm guitar), and a short solo for each mode so guitarists can practice their solos with a "real" band.
_____00000163 Book/CD Pack.....................$17.95

Guitar Tuning For The Complete Idiot (For Smart People Too)*
Centerstream Publications
By Ron Middlebrook
A complete book on how to tune up. Tuning record included. Contents include: Everything You Need To Know About Tuning – with several methods explained; Intonation – what it is and how to set your guitar up; Strings – How To Find The Right Ones For You; 12 String Tuning; Picks; and much more.
_____00000002 ....$5.95

Survival Licks & Bar Room Tricks*
by Mark & J.R.
Centerstream Publications
A survival guide for today's music scene – from learning how to solo in a variety of styles to how to protect yourself from flying bottles. After reading this book, you will be equipped with the knowledge and confidence it takes to pull any gig off. Includes country, blues, rock, metal and jazz fusion licks in notes and tab.
_____00000133 ....$8.95

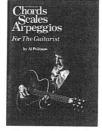

The Complete Book Of Chords, Scales, Arpeggios For The Guitar*
by Al Politano
Centerstream Publications
Every chord, scale and arpeggio is plotted out in every practical position and with some dedicated study, one could play all of them in every position and in all keys. Written with just a minimum amount of verbalization. Use this book for improvisation, studying or playing exercises. This is the best, most complete reference book you can buy.
_____00000021 ....$8.95

Open Guitar Tunings*
Centerstream Publications
The only book that illustrates over 75 different tunings in easy-to-read diagrams. Includes tunings used by artists such as Chet Atkins, Michael Hedges, Jimmy Page, Joe Satriani and more for rock, blues, bluegrass, folk and country styles including open D (for slide guitar), Em, open C, modal tunings and many more.
_____ 00000130 ....$4.95

Over The Top
by Dave Celentano
Centerstream Publications
A new book/CD pack by Dave Celentano for guitarists who want to concentrate on their 2-hand tapping tech-nique.
_____00000166 Book/CD Pack......................$17.95

P.O. Box 17878 - Anaheim Hills, CA 92807   (714) - 779-9390